One More Brown Bag

One More Brown Bag

(of sermons for children)

by
Jerry Marshall Jordan
Illustrated by Mary Lou Anderson

The Pilgrim Press
Cleveland, Ohio

The Pilgrim Press, Cleveland, Ohio 44115

© 1983 by The Pilgrim Press

Printed in the United States of America on acid-free paper

97 96 95 94 93 92   10 9 8 7 6 5

Library of Congress Cataloging-in-Publication Data

Jordan, Jerry Marshall, 1937–
One more brown bag (of sermons for children)

Summary: Fifty-two sermons emphasizing involvement in the
worship of the church and Christian teachings about God and
Jesus.
1. Children sermons.   [1. Sermons.   2. Christian life]
I. Anderson, Mary Lou, ill.   II. Title.
BV4315.J69   1983   252'.53   82-24694
ISBN 0-8298-0645-8 (pbk.)

For Joella and John

Contents

Preface

This volume completes the trilogy of the Brown Bag sermons for children. The first, *The Brown Bag,* and the second, *Another Brown Bag,* have been well received, and I am appreciative. As the Preacher of Ecclesiastes wrote, however, "Of making many books there is no end," so it is with me, with sermons for children and the books that contain them.

Recently I completed a survey of five hundred pastors, selected at random from the United Church of Christ, the United Presbyterian Church in the U.S.A., the Lutheran Church of America, the United Methodist Church, and the American Baptist Churches, asking them to share their opinions and concerns about sermons for children. A majority were very positive about this homiletical genre. It is apparent that there is a vital interest in children's sermons.

Of course, some responded negatively. One said, "Doing children's sermons just isn't my bag." Others said: "It interferes with the worship; it is too often (referring to others, of course!) not well enough thought out theologically; it isn't a comfortable thing to do; it puts the children on display; or, it is something I don't believe in." I don't share these feelings, though I appreciate the honesty. A negative answer is useful nevertheless, helping to evaluate where the problems are with sermons for children and how these problems might be avoided.

As for the positive reactions, the majority of respondents felt they were seeking to obtain an involvement of the children in the worship of the church, to relate personally to the children as their pastor, to teach them about God and Jesus, and to help them feel special. While these certainly validate sermons for children within the worshiping community of faith, even more important is what Jesus said: "Let the children come to me, and do not hinder them; for to such belongs the kingdom of heaven." This has been my rationale, and in this hope and spirit I share these sermons.

My thanks to Gayle, who carefully read each sermon, making suggestions that greatly improved the original copy. Tap and Suzanne, our two children, also shared in this process, even more than they realized. Again I thank Mary Lou Anderson, whose artwork makes this an attractive book. And to my two readers, P. Roy Brammell and Lavonne Eliason, a deep sense of gratitude for taking the time and for expending the thoughtful energy to check the linguistic mechanics. And once more, to the children of the First Congregational Church, United Church of Christ, of Colorado Springs, I thank you—you are special!

Now, let us open *One More Brown Bag.*

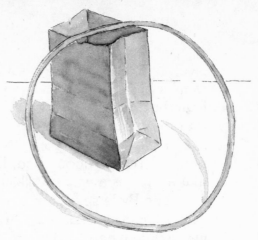

No. 1

More Than a Circle

What I've brought this morning I couldn't get into my brown bag. It's too big. So I did the next best thing. I tore the bag apart and wrapped it around this big thing. And I used more than one bag. I used four.

Where is it? Oh, it's still behind the pulpit. Let me get it. Or better yet, let me roll it out.

Want to guess what's under the brown bag wrapping paper? What's big and round and something you like to play with? That's right, there's only one answer, at least only one I can think of.

A hula-hoop.

You never thought you'd see one of these in church, right? Neither did I. But here it is.

I know that some of you are really good with the hula-hoop, because I've seen some of you use it. Just by the look on your faces, I'd say that lots of you have one. How many do? My, that's quite a few!

Also, by the look on your faces, a questioning look, I get the feeling that you're wondering if I'm going to demonstrate how well I hula with this hoop. Now, I ask you, wouldn't that look funny, me doing that—here? And with this long black robe on? That's one of the funniest things I can think of. I know you'd laugh, and your parents would laugh too.

Tell you what, right after church, you meet me out in front of the church, on the church lawn—oh, give me a few minutes to say hello to your parents and to take off this black robe—and I'll show you how well I can hula with this hoop. You'll laugh, I know, for this isn't my sport.

Well, if I'm not going to do it now, why did I bring it? To talk about God. Did it ever occur to you that a circle is a way of talking about God?

The Bible speaks of God as being "from everlasting to everlasting." In other words, there never was a time when God wasn't, nor will there ever be a time when God won't be. God is forever. "In the beginning God" is the way the Bible begins, and throughout the Bible God is spoken of as being forever and ever. This means we don't talk about God beginning or ending.

Look again at this circle. Where does it begin, and where does it end? Those are questions you don't ask of a circle. It just goes on and on and on. It's only natural that we would see in the circle a good reminder of God.

What this says to us—aside from the fact that there is no end to God—is that God is always with us. The circle reminds us that there is no end to God in our lives. You see, God keeps coming around to us— with a love that is ever encircling us.

No, God isn't a great big circle; rather, the circle reminds us of God.

That's why I brought this big hula-hoop— correction—circle this morning. Whenever you see a circle, think of God, of how God is forever and ever, and how God's love is encircling you even now.

Let us pray.
Dear God: Thank you for being without end, and for your love that never ends. Amen.

No. 2

A Security Blanket

While rummaging through the attic this week, I found something that brought back memories. It's now in my brown bag—a blanket.

This isn't mine. It belongs to my son, who hasn't seen it since he was just a little fellow. It was his security blanket. This reminds me of the one I had when I was very young.

What is a security blanket? It's that blanket that makes us feel secure. What does this word secure mean? It means safe, or OK.

Have you read, or had read to you, the cartoon "Peanuts"? In that cartoon strip—which happens to be one of my favorites—one of the characters, Linus, has a security blanket. Everywhere he goes, it goes. He feels better when it's with him.

That was me. To this day I can remember the blanket's warmth as well as the coolness of the satin edging. Oh, it was so nice to touch. When I went to bed, it cuddled with me, and wherever I went around the house, it dragged behind me.

Maybe you have a security blanket. That's OK. We all need to feel secure on the inside. Right?

Of course, it doesn't have to be a blanket. For myself, now that I no longer have my own security blanket, there are other ways I find security. One way is knowing I can talk to my parents, knowing that they care about me and for me. You can do the same.

Another way of feeling this way comes from friends, those I can trust, those who love me in spite of what I do, those who will be there to help me when I need them. Surely you have friends like that too.

Another kind of security I value is the church. Here I learn about what is right and good and meaningful in life, about Jesus and what Jesus means to us. Because of this, the church makes me feel more secure. The same can be so for you.

But I feel most secure because of God. In the Bible, God says, "Fear not, for I am with you, be not dismayed, for I am your God; . . . I will help you." That's God's promise to me, which gives me a lot of peace of mind and security. And God promises the same to you. Because God does this for us, we can say, "We're in good hands."

Of all the securities in the world, the one God gives you and me is the best. Jesus wanted us to understand this. In all he said and did, he wanted people to realize they could trust God. He trusted God completely. When he died, those who killed him said, "He trusts in God." And he did. So can we. In God is our security. God helps us to feel OK.

Security blankets are OK. But as you grow older, it is my hope and prayer that God's loving care will mean more and more to you. In that is our security— the peace that is beyond all understanding.

Let us pray.

Dear God: Help us to know that you are always with us. Amen.

No. 3

What Are You Worth?

Here's my brown bag. And inside it is another brown bag. And that brown bag is the one I used last week. Am I going to talk about last week's bag today?

When I sat down with you last week, I noticed what was written on the outside of my brown bag. Let me show you what it says.

I'M
WORTH
3¢

In other words, that's what this brown bag is worth if we were to take it back to the supermarket. Why?

We need to save paper. You see, paper comes from trees that have been cut down, chopped up, smashed flat, and rolled out into paper. If we save our paper, we save on the number of trees we have to cut down. That's why there is the need to recycle—reuse—our bags, newspapers, and other paper products.

Notice the note at the bottom of the bag.

RE-USE ME TO SACK
YOUR GROCERIES

What struck me wasn't so much the idea of using this bag again—which, by the way, I think is a good idea (the more bags we save, the more trees we save). Rather, what caught my eye—and I've been thinking about it all week—is the worth of this bag. If it's worth three cents, what are we worth?

I'm told I'm worth a little over five dollars at today's prices. That means if all the elements in my body—like salt, sugar, iron (that's right, there's some iron in me), plus a lot of other things—were taken out (and if they were taken out of me, I wouldn't be alive anymore), they could be sold for a little over five dollars. And the same is true for you, though you'd probably go for a little under five dollars because you're smaller than I am. That makes sense, doesn't it?

But is that all we're worth, just a few dollars? I think not. You're worth more than money, and so am I. We're all very precious. In fact, it's wrong to put a dollar sign on us, for we're not for sale.

What makes you so precious? Your parents can tell you why. And so can I. You're each one of a kind. You're unique—that's another word for special. We love you.

And you are even more precious—valuable beyond money—because God loves you. Believe me, this makes you worth more than all the money in the world.

That's why Jesus said, "Let the children come to me, and do not hinder them; for to such belongs the kingdom of heaven."

When someone asks you what you're worth, just say, "I'm worth everything to God."

Let us pray.
Dear God: Your love makes us feel so valuable! Amen.

No. 4

More Bounce

Good morning!
     Really, now, is it a good morning? It is for me. But I've had mornings that weren't so good, mornings that affected the rest of the day. Has that happened to you?

What are we talking about?

It's a feeling we have, and feelings aren't so easy to pin down. Sad may be one word we could use to explain it. Gloomy is another word. Upset might be the word for how we feel.

Have you ever tried to tell a friend or a brother or a sister or even Mom and Dad how you feel when you don't feel so good. I'm not talking about when you're sick—that's bad enough. I'm talking about when you're unhappy. Try it sometime. I have, and it helps.

Yesterday I was playing ball with Suzanne, and as we bounced the ball back and forth, I thought,

"Sometimes we feel like that ball when all the air is out of it." I have her ball in my brown bag.

Let me tell you a little about this ball. Suzanne received it for her birthday. This ball is used for the game "Four Square." It's made of rubber, and when it's full of air it can really bounce. I found that out yesterday.

But the day before yesterday this ball wouldn't bounce at all. It was like it is now—flat. You see, it had two holes in it, holes made by stickers. We pumped it up, and in a matter of minutes it went flat. We couldn't play with it, and that made us unhappy. A ball is to have fun with, to bounce and bounce and bounce.

That's us too. Sometimes we feel flat. We don't bounce as we should. We're sad or gloomy or upset— we're unhappy.

I fixed this ball. Notice the patches—two of them. Now this ball will hold the air I put in it. And with this pump, I'm going to do just that—pump it up.

We need to be patched, too, when troubles flatten our happiness. That's why we come to church each Sunday to learn how God loves us. This helps us to bounce again with joy.

No, I'm not talking about us bouncing like this ball does. I mean we become happy on the inside.

I like what the Bible says about this: "I know that there is nothing better for them to be happy and enjoy themselves as long as they live; . . . it is God's gift to [them]." That's talking about us and about how God wants to bring happiness into our lives.

Happiness happens when we learn that we are loved, and it makes us feel good when we love others. Bounce that thought around a bit.

Let us pray.
Dear God: Fill us with your love. Amen.

No. 5

It's Time To . . .

What's that noise?
Is it an alarm clock?
But where is it?
In my brown bag?
How did it get there?
Why is it ringing now?

I have to be honest with you. It's my alarm clock, and I not only put it in my brown bag, I also set it to ring at this time.

You know what? I don't like alarm clocks. Never have. The sound alarms me, even when I'm awake. But when I'm sleeping deeply, when I'm dreaming beautiful dreams, this ring in my ear is very alarming.

Do you like that sound?

How many of you have an alarm clock? Is it set each night?

The purpose of this kind of clock is to wake us up so we can start doing what we need to do.

What this says about us—when we set our alarm clocks—is that we can be counted on. We're responsible. Instead of lying in bed, sleeping on and on as if it didn't matter what we did, we get up and get started. That's good. Think of what our world would be like if there weren't any alarm clocks to wake people up. Oh, I guess we'd get up, but because there are just so many hours in a day, it stands to reason we wouldn't get as much done. And that's not so good.

19

But there's more to this clock than the alarm, as you can see. Count with me, starting with one. . . . And we've come all the way around to twelve. That's how many hours we have on the face of this clock. Double that, and we have the number of hours in a day. Twenty-four. That's all we have in a day—no more, no less. Eight to twelve hours of that time are used for sleeping. This leaves from twelve to sixteen hours to dress, eat, travel here and there, work, play, read, watch television, and do all the other things we find ourselves doing.

The clock should remind us that we have a lot to do. The question is whether we'll get up and get done what needs to be done. We can't do everything, but we can (at least, this is what I keep telling myself) do more than we do. Each of us has the same amount of time. It's very important how we use the time we have.

And it matters to God too. Time is God's gift to us. In the Bible it says of the gift, "Nothing can be added to it, nor anything taken from it; God has made it so."

I'm glad my clock has an alarm, even though I don't like the way it sounds. You see, I need to be reminded to get going. I want to use wisely the gift of time God has given me. And I want to encourage you to do the same. Think about how you can do this in a way that will please God, who gave you time to begin with. Time isn't to be wasted, especially when there's so much good we can be doing.

Let us pray.
Dear God: Help us to use our time well. Amen.

No. 6

Love Is Warm

Today we talk of love. It's Valentine's Day.
Yesterday, my love gave me a gift. It's an outdoor thermometer.

I've wanted a thermometer like this for a long time. It's funny, though, I had planned to give her one like this as a Valentine gift. (This tells you how much I really wanted one!) When she realized what I was thinking about—sometimes I talk too much—she told me that she had already gotten one for me. So yesterday she gave it to me—early, before I went shopping.

Isn't it a nice-looking thermometer? The numbers are big enough to read from a distance. That's important. You see, I want to put this thermometer on a tree in my backyard so I can tell from the window how cold or warm it is.

I wish I had had this thermometer a few days ago. It got so cold school was canceled that day. How cold did it get? The report was nineteen degrees below zero. Now that's cold! And with the wind the chill factor (my son used to call it the "chili factory") went down to minus thirty. That's *cold*! And the weather report across most of the nation was cold, oh, so cold! In Wisconsin, it got down to fifty below—and that was without the wind. That's almost as low as this thermometer will go. This says minus sixty. I hope it never gets that cold here.

I like cold weather, but not a lot of it—just enough to remind me how I love warm weather. How warm? Oh, say, around seventy to seventy-five degrees. That I love.

Speaking of love, have you ever thought of love and weather? I often do. For example, when it gets cold we think a lot about keeping ourselves warm. There's nothing wrong with doing that, except when we hug only ourselves and not others. This isn't related just to the weather. It also has to do with how selfish we get sometimes. That's when our love really cools.

When we hear the saying "It's a cold world out there!" that's not so much talking about the weather as about how unloving some people are—like being uncaring, thoughtless, cruel. There's too much of that kind of coldness in our world.

Have you ever felt like someone gave you a cold shoulder? That means someone didn't want to have much to do with you. This hurts, especially when it's someone you care a lot about. Have you given someone else a cold shoulder? It's not a very loving thing to do.

The warmth of friendship is nice when we love one another with a love that really cares.

In the Bible, God says, "My heart . . . my compassion grows warm." And that's what God is telling us to do—let our hearts grow warm with love. Our world needs to be warmed that way—with love. For this reason I now put a big heart on the front of this thermometer. Let us do all we can to make this a warmer world—and I'm not talking about the weather.

Let us pray.

Dear God: Warm our hearts and help us to warm the hearts of others. Amen.

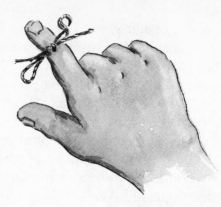

No. 7

Don't Forget

"Don't forget!"
How many times have I heard that! And for good reason. I have a tendency to forget. Sometimes I wonder about myself. It's not that I want to forget—I just do! Perhaps I think about too many things at once.

Does that happen to you? Do people say, "Oh, you forgot!"

Has anyone ever said to you, "Tie a string around your finger"? Tying a string around your finger is supposed to remind you not to forget. You see the string and it makes you wonder why you tied it there in the first place. That will remind you of what you're not supposed to forget.

Have you ever tried that? Did it work? The times I tried it, it helped.

Emily, put your hand out. I don't know if you have the problem of forgetting—I hope you don't—I'm going to tie a string around your finger. Hold still. There. And I'm also going to tie one around my own finger (which isn't so easy when you try to do it yourself—that's why it's best if someone gives you a helping hand). I want you to remember some important things to do. I'm not thinking of things like making your bed or brushing your teeth, as important as such things are. I'm thinking of some other things.

Don't forget to thank a friend who has gone out

of his or her way to do something nice for you. I'm sad when I think of the times when I forgot to do this—not on purpose, but just because I began to think about other things. So you may want to tie a string around your finger and not take it off until that friend has been thanked.

Don't forget to remind yourself how important it is to be honest and fair with others. We hear almost every day, "It doesn't matter. You've got to look out for yourself." Well, it does matter what we do. Why? We're not supposed to take advantage of others. So tie that string and be honest and fair, for this matters a lot.

Don't forget to read your Bible every day. I know some of you are still learning to read or haven't yet learned. So have your parents read the stories about Jesus and the other great people of the Bible. Above all, read what Jesus said about God. Tie a string on your finger and read your Bible.

Don't forget to say your prayers. It's so easy to go to bed and forget to tell God what's on your mind. You need to be still so God can talk to you through your thoughts too. This is something I try never to forget, but I have to admit there have been times when sleep came first. Saying our prayers is one of the most important things we do each day. So tie that string on your finger and pray more—and it doesn't have to be just at bedtime.

I have a bag of strings for you. Take one. Tie it on your finger so you won't forget the important things we talked about this morning.

In the Bible it says, "Remember and do not forget."

Let us pray.
Dear God: Help us to remember what's important. Amen.

No. 8

Symbols of Life

What is a symbol?
It's something that points beyond itself to something else. This ring on my finger, for example, is a symbol, telling all who see it that I'm married. So it's more than a ring. It's a way of telling something about me without words.

Let's talk about some symbols of life we see each day.

Here's one—a tree. A tree is a symbol of life. In springtime and summertime the trees have green leaves all over them. When the weather gets colder, the trees lose their leaves. But when it gets warmer, as it does in April and May, the leaves come back again. Those leaves help the tree grow. All this reminds us of life. So the tree, with all its leaves, stands as a symbol of life.

Another symbol of life is water. They say, "Where there's water there's life." Isn't that true? Have you ever noticed how a plant perks up when it is watered after being dry for several days? Yes, water is a symbol of life. Without it, we and all other living things wouldn't live.

And here's another symbol in my brown bag: a Rubik's Cube. Ah, the look on your faces asks "How is this a symbol of life?"

Do you know how it works? Of course you do, at least those of you who have one. It's not easy.

It has six sides and six colors, and when the puzzle is solved, all the blue squares will be on one side, the red squares will be on another side. As for the green, orange, white, and yellow squares, they too will be on the side to which they belong. Each side of the cube has nine squares in three rows, and the rows can be turned this way and that way, or that way and this way, or. . . . That's why it's so difficult. There are over three billion possible moves we can make in an attempt to solve the puzzle. That's a lot. I can't even count that high. People who can solve the puzzle say it takes only a few key moves made at the right time and in the right way to solve it.

Right now, the world record for solving this puzzle is 25.6 seconds. Wow! And I can't even do it in a day. I have to be honest—I haven't yet solved Rubik's Cube. By the way, there are several books out (one written by a thirteen-year-old boy) on how to solve Rubik's Cube.

For me Rubik's Cube is a symbol of life. You see, in life we can move in so many ways, in so many directions. I'm not thinking about how we move physically, with our bodies, though that could be considered. I'm thinking of all the decisions we have to make. Will we do it this way or that way? What is the right way or the wrong way to do something? There are many, many, many decisions we have to make in life. Thus life is a puzzle we try to solve. That's why I see this as a symbol of life.

Life's puzzle takes a lot longer than 25.6 seconds to solve. It takes a lifetime of living. But there is a book that can tell us the right turns to make. It's the Bible. In it are the answers we need if we are to make right decisions in our lives. Read it, and learn how to solve life's many puzzling problems.

Let us pray.
Dear God: Help us to solve life's puzzle of how best to live. Amen.

No. 9

A Knotty Problem

Life has a lot of little problems. Here's one that bugs me.

I'll be walking along, and my shoelace becomes untied. Does that ever happen to you? What is even more upsetting is retying the lace, only to have it come loose again. This doesn't happen to me now as much as it used to, when I was your age. I now tie it tighter. I can remember, when I was very young, asking a big person to tie my shoelace with a double knot. Do you ever do that?

But there's another problem with shoelaces that bugs me, even now that I'm a big person. Let me show you what I mean. In my brown bag I have a shoe. I start to tie it, thinking that I want it to stay tied. I pull the string extra hard. Oops! It broke.

That's one of the little problems that really gets me. Usually it happens when I'm in a hurry. Or when I retie it, the knot is where it is uncomfortable, pressing down on the tongue of my shoe and on the top of my foot. It's as if I have a small rock pressing down on the tongue of my shoe. You know the feeling.

When this happens, there's only one thing to do, until a pair of new shoelaces can be purchased, and that's retie it so it doesn't hurt and go on. It reminds me of the saying that when you come to the end of your rope, you tie a knot and hang on. In other words, don't give up. So it is with this shoelace. Tie the knot and go on. Don't let a little shoelace get the best of you.

It's the same with all the little problems of life, like misplaced glasses or spilled milk or a skinned knee or a broken pencil or . . . there are so many little problems we could list.

Those problems usually don't seem little at the time. They are most upsetting. But they are really little problems. And as I showed you, the thing to do is figure out what to do about the problem, get it done, and then get on with the more important things in life.

In the Bible, there are these words: "perplexed, but not driven to despair." Perplexed? That's a big word, and it means puzzled or full of questions or beside oneself. Paul, the man who said those words (you've heard his name before, because he is a very important person in the Bible), wasn't talking about the little problems of life, like a broken shoelace. Sure, he must have had many little problems, and maybe a broken shoelace was one of them. But his main concern was with the big problems. I know he would agree, though, that the little ones can be most perplexing. And despair? That is another big word, and it means that one is about to give up. That's what we must not do. We must not despair and give up.

Remember, we have a helpful promise from God, found in the Bible: "For I, the Lord your God say to you, 'Fear not, I will help you.' "

No, God will not tie our shoelaces for us, but God most certainly will help us when we are troubled with life's many problems, the big ones as well as the little ones.

Let us pray.
Dear God: Thank you for helping us.

No. 10

Pointing, the Wrong Way

Have you ever had a finger pointed at you like this? I sure have. In fact, at times I've felt as if that accusing finger was bigger than life, as big as the one in my brown bag.

This hand, with the index finger pointed, is about two feet long and made out of posterboard. It's certainly big enough to help us remember what we are talking about this morning.

By the way, what does the word accuse mean? It means to blame someone for something: "You did it!" or "It's your fault!"

I might add that at times the person who pointed at me was right and I was wrong—in the wrong. I needed to be told I was wrong, though it never was much fun being told. And it never did much good to tell me unless the person pointing the finger loved me, or at least cared about me. Only then did I know that what was being said was for my own good. Then and only then did I take to heart the advice given.

I can also remember when I was pointed at and it wasn't my fault. It was my brother's or sister's fault, or someone else's fault. Have you ever had that happen to you?

Here are two things to consider.

The first is that maybe you have misunderstood your brother or your sister or your friend. Maybe he or she has better reasons than you realize for doing what you think is questionable. Before the blame is pointed out, you need to get the facts, for you may be wrong.

29

Be careful about this.

Second, before you point that accusing finger, ask yourself if that's something you've done too, or are now doing. Are you accusing your sister or brother of not having her or his room cleaned up, when yours isn't clean either? Or are you claiming that a friend stayed too long on the swing at school, when the day before you stayed on the swing twice as long? Or are you crying about being hit by another child, claiming you were just standing there, when you really hit first?

Have you ever noticed that when we point like this, we have three fingers pointing back at ourselves? This can remind us of what Jesus was talking about when he said, "Why do you see the speck that is in your brother's eye, but do not notice the log that is in your own eye?" Isn't that a funny thing—a log in someone's eye? Jesus must have smiled when he said that, but he was very serious, meaning: Maybe we're just as much at fault, if not more, than the person we're blaming. Think about it the next time you see those three fingers pointing back at you.

Really, it's best not to point at all. Jesus said, "Judge not." When we point an accusing finger, it's usually a judging finger. Is this the best way to deal with others? I don't think so. It would be better if we were to take that accusing, judging, scolding finger and turn it back into our hand. Then put your hand on the other person's shoulders, saying, "How can I help you?" or "It's not easy, is it?" or "Let's talk about this" or even "Let's work it out."

This is what Jesus did. And it's what he wants us to do too, every time we feel the need to point a finger at someone else.

Let us pray.
Dear God: Forgive us for pointing in the wrong way. Amen.

No. 11

Divine Math

Let me check your math. Do you know how to add and subtract? That's what they teach in school, isn't it? That's what they taught me long ago.

I don't claim to be a whiz in mathematics, especially when I get into what they call higher math. But I did learn to add and subtract. We even had contests, when the teacher would divide the class into two teams and we'd go to the board to see who could solve the math problems first.

We're not going to have a contest here. That would be fun, but I'll let your teacher do that. For now, just call out the answers as I show you the flash cards. Ready?

First, addition:

$$
\begin{array}{ccccccc}
7 & 4 & 3 & 5 & 1 & 6 & 7 \\
+1 & +3 & +7 & +2 & +6 & +1 & +7 \\
\hline
\end{array}
$$

Very good.

Now, subtraction:

$$
\begin{array}{ccccccc}
7 & 8 & 5 & 4 & 7 & 8 & 7 \\
-1 & -1 & -5 & -1 & -2 & -7 & -7 \\
\hline
\end{array}
$$

Very good.

Have you learned to multiply? Some of you have. For those of you who haven't learned this kind of math, it's a short way of adding. Let me show you what these flash cards look like. Those of you who

31

know how to multiply can give the answers. The × is
the sign for multiplying, and we call it "times." I'm
going to do just the sevens. Ready?

7	7	7	7	7	7	7
×1	×2	×3	×4	×5	×6	×7

Very fine.

Do you think Jesus knew his math? Sure he did.
He went to school too. But there's something else
Jesus learned which goes beyond math, and it's very
important.

One day Peter, one of Jesus' closest friends,
asked, "Lord, how often shall my brother sin against
me, and I forgive him? As many as seven times?"

Before I give Jesus' answer, I'll ask you, "Would
you forgive your brother or sister or anyone seven
times?" If you're like me, you'd say, as I have, "Seven
times! That's too many times. Once, yes; twice, maybe;
but seven times? No way." We tend to want to get
even instead of forgiving—right?

Here's Jesus' answer: "I do not say to you seven
times, but seventy times seven." Wow! That multiplies
out to 490 times. Think of it—to forgive someone that
many times! How can we? Impossible.

Wait a minute. Jesus isn't saying we are to forgive
that many times. Rather, this is Jesus' way of saying we
are to forgive every time people ask us for our
forgiveness. Even if they wrong us on the 491st time,
we're to forgive them if they ask us. This means we're
to forgive again and again and again, without ever
saying no.

Wouldn't we want someone to do that for us? Of
course.

This isn't school math, this is divine math. It's not
taught in the public schools, but it's taught in your
church school. There you and I learn what Jesus
taught. We learn how God wants us to act toward

those who have wronged us. This is how God acts toward us when we do wrong and ask for forgiveness.

But how can we forgive so many times? We can, if we're willing and loving, and if we allow God to help us.

Let us pray.
Dear God: Help us to be forgiving of others again and again and again. Amen.

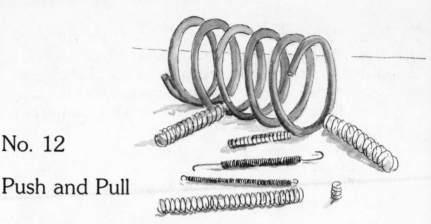

No. 12

Push and Pull

Yesterday was the first day of spring. So what do I have in my brown bag today? Springs.

Springs? Yes, big springs and little springs, as well as middle-sized springs.

Obviously I'm making a play on words. The spring that came yesterday is the name of a season, the time of year which comes after winter in our part of the world, the months of March, April, and May. The springs in my brown bag are made of curly pieces of metal. The two words sound alike, that's for sure, and one reminds me of the other. Let me explain.

First, there's the metal spring. I have a fondness for these funny-looking pieces of metal, all curled and wound up as they are. In my garage, where I found these springs, I have a lot more. Why so many? You never know when you'll need one. The purpose of a spring is to push out when pressed inward, or to pull inward when stretched out. And it keeps on doing this again and again. A spring has power to push and pull. What would we do in our world if we didn't have springs? Certainly a lot of our machines wouldn't work.

Then there's the season of the year: springtime. This is when the trees begin to get their leaves, when we plant our gardens and flowers and they begin to grow. The grass is already starting to turn green. People say, "Spring has sprung."

This is how I connect these two words—spring

and spring. In nature, in the growing of plants, there seems to be a power at work, pushing and pulling new life into being. Already there are some little purple flowers in my backyard, called crocuses, which seem to have just sprung up out of the ground. I know and you know that there isn't any spring like this metal one down underneath the ground pushing them up. But there is a force that's pushing them up each year at this time, along with the warm sun pulling on them. The same is true with the grass, leaves, vegetables, and all kinds of seasonal plants. They begin to spring up and grow.

Now can you see why one kind of spring always reminds me of the other? Yes, they sound alike, and there's a power here that causes me to think of one and then the other.

But there's a difference. The kind of spring I'm holding in my hand is made by people. The power that makes the season, the springtime, is God's. God is the force at work here, ever pulling and pushing new life into being.

In the Bible it says:

Faithfulness will spring up from the ground,
    and righteousness will look down from the sky.
Yea, the Lord will give what is good,
    and our land will yield its increase.

That's the way God works in the springtime.

Let us pray.

Dear God: For all you do in nature, we thank you. Amen.

No. 13

Be Holy

From my brown bag—a sheet of paper and a hole puncher. Let me show you how these two things go together.

I'll hold the paper over the bag so I won't have bits of paper all over the carpet. To let them fall where I punch them out wouldn't be very neat, and the janitor wouldn't like that very much. Here goes.

What am I doing? I'm punching holes. I'm being holey!

We hear the word holy a lot around the church. Of course, I'm using two words that sound alike but are spelled differently. When I punch my piece of paper, the word is H-O-L-E-Y. The word we hear in church is spelled H-O-L-Y.

Being holy—H-O-L-Y—means what? Any ideas?

When we say God is holy, what are we saying? That we can see through God? No, that would be spelled H-O-L-E-Y. One of our favorite hymns is "Holy, Holy, Holy, Lord God Almighty." Here's this word again—H-O-L-Y—three times in a row. What we're saying is that God is God and there is no other God. One part of this great hymn says, "Only thou art holy, there is none beside thee." Our God is so great, so marvelous, so wonderful, so powerful, so all-knowing, so everywhere, so . . . well, we just have to say *holy*. In this sense we're saying that God is the highest and the best of everything there is. The Bible speaks of God as being holy.

I've heard people called holy too. Have you? What does that mean? That they are like God? No. It means "being set apart to the service of God." You see, God has a will for us, that we should be ever so loving, ever so caring, and ever so helpful to others. When we do that, the holy God is in our thoughts and in our hearts. Then we begin to act like God wants us to act. That's when we become holy. That doesn't mean we are like God, but it does mean that the holy God is in us.

I'm using the word "we" as I talk about this word holy. Do you think it's a word for us? Can we be holy? Sure we can, and we are holy when we are set apart for God—when we become doers of God's will.

How can we become holy? One way is by being examples of right living. We don't do this to show off, as if we each were saying by our actions, "Look how good I am!" Rather, we know what is right and what is wrong, and we choose the right instead of the wrong. If we do this because we love God, we don't want to stand on top of the church and shout it out to everyone. Let our actions say it for us. "Holy."

Another way is to become more and more open to God, by praying, by reading the Bible, by coming to church—all ways of coming closer to God. Again, this isn't for show, to make others think we're better than we are. No, if we do this for the right reason—to come closer to God—then we're doing what is right. The nearer we get to God, or the nearer we allow God to get to us, the more others will see the happiness in our lives and in our faces. Let our joy say it for us. "Holy."

A third way to become holy is the way of love—being ever more loving. In the Bible it says, "Let your light so shine . . . that [others] may see your good works and give glory to [God]." That means being loving, and let this be said of us: "Holy."

Yes, we can be holy—"set apart to the service of God."

Let us pray.
Dear God: Help us to be holy. Amen.

No. 14

Throw It Away

I think you'd have trouble guessing what's in my brown bag this morning, even if I gave you a thousand guesses. So I'll tell you.

It's a wastebasket.

I've had this wastebasket for about twenty years. It has been under my desk all that time.

Just think how much wastepaper has gone into this little basket over the years. If it were all piled up, how much would it be? Would there be enough to fill up a garage? Would the pile be as high as our sanctuary ceiling? That would be a pile sixty-five feet high. Of course, I'm glad I don't have all that trash, but the thought of it makes me wonder.

I am thankful for this wastebasket. What if I didn't have it, or one like it? Would all the trash just be thrown in the corner? That wouldn't be good! Knowing me, I'd probably get a brown bag or two and fill them up. Anyway, I'm glad to have this nice-looking wastebasket.

This wastebasket has a message for us: There are a lot of things we need to throw away.

For sure, we all have a lot of trash to throw away. We are reminded of this especially when Mom looks under our beds, in our closets, or in our playrooms. But enough talk about that. This wastebasket reminds us that there are other things in our lives we need to throw away. For example:

39

- mean, hateful thoughts
- bad habits, like being late or not picking up after ourselves
- not-so-nice words
- smart-aleck replies
- moments of laziness

And the list could go on and on.

These things are a lot different from wastepaper. And to throw away what we've been talking about, you don't use a wastebasket. I know that. But this wastebasket is a good reminder for us to throw away what isn't needed, or what isn't good, in our lives. And we all have that kind of stuff in our lives. We need to do something about getting rid of it. That's what God wants us to do. But how do we do that?

Make your wastebasket—you probably have one in your room—the reminder to throw out those things that aren't doing you any good.

If you are like me, you'll need help. I still have too much stuff—not only in my study but also in my life. We can throw wastepaper away by ourselves, but when it comes to bad habits, we need help.

And we have help from God.

God wants us to throw out those things in our lives that keep us from being good and feeling OK about ourselves.

In the Bible it says, "For everything there is a . . . time for every matter under heaven," and then in the long list of the things this includes, it says, "a time to keep, and a time to cast away."

Let us pray.

Dear God: We need your help to throw away our bad habits. Amen.

No. 15

Crosses

Crosses. Today I have a bag full of crosses.
Here's a cross that usually hangs in my
office. Notice how pretty it is. It looks like gold, but it's
brass. Notice how long and slender the lines of this
cross are. I enjoy looking at it.

Here's another one that's not so enjoyable. Do
you know what it's made of? Barbed wire. That's the
kind of wire they use on fences in order to keep cattle
from getting out of the field. It has barbs on it, little
sharp pieces of metal. They hurt. I know. When I was
a boy on the farm, I fixed barbed-wire fences, and I
often stuck my hand with barbs like these. I made this
cross from some of that wire from my parent's farm.

Here's another cross. This one is made of glass,
the kind of glass that goes into church windows:
stained glass. This was given to me by a friend.

And here's one more cross. This one comes from

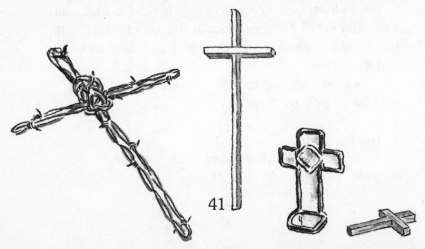

41

Jerusalem and is made of wood. Jesus died on a wooden cross outside the city of Jerusalem long ago.

All these crosses—be they of shiny metal, barbed wire, glass, or wood—make us think of Jesus' cross, and even more of his death.

Why did Jesus die on the cross? That's a big question. Would you like to tell me what you think?

Certainly there were some bad people who caused Jesus to die. There were also some nice people involved who didn't understand what Jesus was saying or what he was doing. They put him to death on a cross on a hill outside Jerusalem.

Jesus didn't stop them. He didn't run and hide. He allowed himself to be put up on that cross because he was willing to die—if that is what it would take—to tell people how much God truly loved them.

You know what? He succeeded. Ever since, we have remembered Jesus and what he said and did, so that we might know more fully what it means to be loved by God.

I don't like the idea that Jesus was killed so that we might know this. But it happened. In the Bible it says, "God shows his love for us in that . . . Christ died for us."

When you go home today, talk with your parents about this and discuss with them how we know even more about God's love because of the cross.

And when you come to church next Sunday and see the big cross on this table in the sanctuary, think about God's love for us and how Jesus died to tell us about it.

If you would like to talk with me about this, I would be happy to do so.

Let us pray.

Dear God: May the cross always remind us of your love. Amen.

No. 16

How Exciting!

Are you excited? "About what?" you ask. About Jesus' coming today.

Today is Palm Sunday. Do you know what happened on that first Palm Sunday?

The Bible tells how Jesus came to the city called Jerusalem. He came there to tell the people about God. Sure, the people who lived there knew about God. They believed and prayed, trying their best to follow the rules God had given them for living better lives. Why then would Jesus come to tell them what they already knew and were trying to do?

Jesus was God's special person, who understood all about God's love. Some thought they knew more about God than Jesus did. But they didn't.

Many who lived in Jerusalem had already heard about Jesus, about the many good things he had done. This caused much excitement when it was reported that he was coming to town. I like the way this is told in the Bible. "When he entered Jerusalem the whole city went wild with excitement."

Many people were excited about his coming, and when at last they saw him, they had to do something or say something, for they couldn't keep their excitement inside. We're told they ran out to meet him. Many began to shout, "Hosanna! Blessings on him who comes in the name of the Lord!" ("Hosanna" means "Save us" or "Help us" or "Keep us safe from those who can harm us.") Many felt Jesus would be a new leader, like a military leader, who would protect them from their enemies. And if he was to be their new leader, at least in their way of thinking, he would then be like a king. So they treated him that way. As he rode on his donkey, some took off their coats and put them on the road for Jesus to ride over (people often did this for kings then). Others tore branches from the palm trees and waved them in the air, shouting "Hosanna!"

Because of those branches, we call it Palm Sunday. And we remember the people's excitement. If we had been there, I know we too would have been excited—enough to have joined that crowd, shouting and waving at the same time.

Why do we get excited today? We don't see Jesus as a military leader coming to protect us from our enemies. We do think of Jesus as a king, and we call him "King of kings." But what excites us now is mainly the realization that Jesus was coming then, and coming even now, to tell us more about God. That's exciting news, good news.

There's a hymn I like: "All Glory, Laud, and Honor." Here are some of its words:

> All glory, laud, and honor
> To thee, Redeemer, King,
> To whom the lips of children
> Make sweet hosannas ring!

That's what I want you to do now—with me. In my brown bag I have some palm branches. Each of you may take one. As the congregation stands and sings this hymn, let's march around the sanctuary shouting "Hosanna" and waving these palms—with excitement—for Jesus came to Jerusalem for us.

Now that we're back, let's pray.

Let us pray.
Dear God: May this day always excite us. Amen.

No. 17

Those Beautiful Butterflies

Did you ever lie on your back out in a meadow and watch the butterflies fly here and there and back again? This has to be one of the most delightful things I have ever done. It's a beautiful experience.

I want to show you the big butterfly I have in my brown bag. How do you like my artwork? This isn't as pretty as the butterflies God makes. I wish I had a real one to show you this morning, but it's too early for butterflies. They appear in warmer weather.

Do you know the story of the butterfly's life? First there's the caterpillar, which lives for a time, eating, eating, and eating. Then it wraps itself up in a chrysalis, which looks like a tiny, brown sleeping bag all closed up. It stops its activities and goes into a deep sleep, being ever so still, as if it had died. Then, when the time is right, it breaks out of its chrysalis as a butterfly. Many of you have learned about this at school.

But why talk about butterflies at church? And why this morning?

Because this is a special morning and butterflies have a special place in the thoughts of this day. Today is Easter. For hundreds and hundreds of years, the butterfly has been used to tell the Easter story. Let me explain.

The caterpillar represents us in this life, the lowly life we live now. Then something happens to the caterpillar. No, it really isn't dead when it wraps itself

45

inside its chrysalis, but because it is so still, it appears lifeless. So we say this is like us when we die. However, it does break out of the chrysalis to become a beautiful butterfly. This is what we call the next life after we have lived the first life and have died. The butterfly reminds us that we'll live again—with God. It doesn't mean that we'll turn into a beautiful butterfly, but rather that our next life will be beautiful to behold.

It was God who allowed Jesus to live again. Jesus was killed, but God raised him up again, and he lives. The butterfly is a way of talking about this, and not only about Jesus but also about us.

The caterpillar probably has no idea that it will become a beautiful butterfly, but we are different. We know what God has promised us. When we die, we will be allowed to live again in a much more beautiful way, to live with God forever. Beautiful!

When you look at a butterfly this summer, think about the beauty God makes possible in that delicate creature. Then think about the thing God will do for us, and what God did for Jesus. Beautiful!

By the way, I have some colorful paper butterflies in my brown bag for each of you to wear.* On them is written, "Jesus lives!" And as you wear your butterfly, say to yourself, "And God will do this for me too." That's . . . so beautiful! . . .

Let us pray.

Dear God: For making Easter such a beautiful experience, we thank you. Amen.

*A curled piece of masking tape, sticky side out, was on the back of each butterfly.

No. 18

Be Sharp

I like pencils. There's a holder on my desk that's full of sharp pencils. I like them sharp.

As far back as I can remember, I've liked pencils of all sizes, even the short ones. The color doesn't matter, just as long as they're sharp. I also like my pencils to have good erasers.

In my opinion, a pencil is no good if it's dull. You know what a dull one is like. It doesn't write very well. And furthermore, I don't think an unsharpened pencil looks very sharp.

That's why I have in my brown bag one of the best of all inventions when it comes to the pencil. Care to guess what it is? Of course! A pencil sharpener.

Isn't this a nice-looking one? It's the kind that sticks to a desk or tabletop. This rubber bottom makes a suction and holds the sharpener in place.

Notice what is even more special about this pencil sharpener. See all these holes of different sizes? They are there because pencils come in different sizes, from fat ones to skinny ones.

When I look across my desk and see all those sharp pencils pointing up, ready to be used, I think, "Be sharp!" If I were to say to you, "Be sharp!" what would I be saying? "Be at your best!"

Here I think of being at my best, of sharpening my love for God, the way Jesus said to: "You shall love the Lord your God with all your heart, and with

47

all your soul, and with all your strength, and with all your mind." That's how I want you to be sharp too.

Be sharp in your heart. In other words, don't allow yourself to be dull toward others. To be dull is not to notice what is troubling them, to be uncaring about them, not to take time enough to be really loving. But that's not the way I want you to act. To be sharp, to act with love—that's when you are at your best, when you are the most willing to love with all your heart.

Be sharp in your soul. Another word for soul is life, or the "life that is within you." It's the self that makes you you. And you (if you're like me) have a problem with yourself, don't you? Sometimes you feel down, you're not happy. Life is dull and not very exciting. You can't be at your best then. This usually happens—I know it does to me—when you don't feel good about yourself. Do you think God wants you to feel this way? No, and the reason is that you're special. God made you special. Ah, to be sharp, to feel your best about yourself—that's when you are the most willing to be your best with all your soul, or self.

Be sharp in your mind. You do that when you use the mind God has given you. Think good thoughts. One of the best ways to do this is by reading—the Bible and other good books—and asking questions of people who know a lot about life. To be sharp, to really use your brains—that's when you are the most willing to learn with all your mind.

Be sharp in your strength. Be strong. Be strong in your body—and this means good exercise and good food. Be strong in your willingness to do what is right, being fair and honest. Be strong in saying "no" to things that are unfair and dishonest. To be sharp, to be strong—that's when you are the most willing to live with all your strength.

Sharp pencils remind us to love God with our very best.

Let us pray.
Dear God: We want to be sharp, to love you with heart, soul, mind and strength. Amen.

No. 19

For Mothers

What I have in my brown bag comes from high in a tree. Care to guess? What else but a nest? Here it is.

I want you to know that I didn't take this nest away from the birds that built it. This is last year's model, and apparently it was no longer in use when it fell out of the tree. That's right, it fell out of a tree in my backyard. Never, never, would I climb a tree and take a nest in use.

Just look at this nest. It's very well built. Notice how the outside is woven together with strong twigs. In fact, there's even a piece of plastic. I wonder if the birds that built it put this plastic among the twigs for decoration. On the inside it's all soft and cuddly, filled with bits of string, grass, and feathers. The way it's shaped, it looks very safe, with high sides making a deep round nest.

I think this is a robin's nest. The birds that built it did a good job. I'm sure it was built with love.

What's a nest for? That's a silly question, isn't it? It's for holding the eggs and then baby birds after they are hatched. It's their home while they're growing up.

When I look at this nest, I think of how warm and safe our homes are. Did that thought occur to you?

I also think of our mothers. Maybe one of the reasons my thoughts go that way is that this is Mother's Day. And what about our fathers? They too are important. Tell you what, we'll give them their special time in a few weeks, on Father's Day. But today . . .

When I look at this nest, the mother bird is the one I think of. Before the eggs are hatched, the mother bird keeps them warm. She does this with loving care. When the eggs hatch, she's there, ready to feed each of the little chirpers. She'll fly away from the nest for only a few minutes at a time—to pick up a worm or a grasshopper or something else to feed her little ones. And she does this with love.

So do our mothers care for us. They are right there when we need them most. When we are hungry, they provide us with the food we need. In short, they care for us with tender, loving care. That's the way my mother did it, and I know that's the way your mothers are doing it for you.

Then there comes the time when the mother bird does what at first glance seems strange. She pushes the birds out of the nest—but not when they're still little, only when they've grown enough to leave the nest and fly on their own. Then she nudges them out. And this too is her way of loving.

When we're old enough, our mothers will also want us to leave home and be on our own. Why? Because only then can we be fully grown, and that's important to us and to her.

Yes, on this Mother's Day let's tell it like it is: We owe more to our mothers than we realize, all because of their love for us. So today we need to tell them how much we love them and to thank them for being so good to us. Obey that part of the Fifth Commandment which says "Honor . . . your mother."

Let us pray.
Dear God: For our mothers and their loving care, we thank you. Amen.

No. 20

It Boomerangs

The prop that's in my brown bag this morning comes from a faraway place called Australia. No, it isn't a kangaroo, it's—a boomerang.

This one was given to me last week by a friend who had recently visited that country on the other side of the world. I'm so pleased. I've always wanted one.

What do you do with this funny-shaped stick? You throw it and then hope it comes back to you. That's right. If thrown correctly, it will turn in the air and return to you.

Some people practice doing this and become very good at it. Some even enter contests. I heard of someone who threw and caught a boomerang twelve times without moving one step. That's not easy. It takes practice—a lot of practice.

I just want to throw it for fun. I've read the instructions. Place it in the palm of the hand with a firm grip, making sure the flat side is facing outward, with the other end directly in front of the thrower. (I've got to stand up to do this right.) Then, when holding it like this, the arm is to be raised to the ten o'clock position, flicking the wrist as it's thrown. It's best always to throw it into and a little right of the wind.

Ready?

You thought I was going to throw it! No, not here—not with all these people out there ready to duck and with all that beautiful stained glass up there.

But I want to sit down and talk to you a bit more about this boomerang.

We're like boomerangs. By this, I mean that what we do often comes back to us. Consider, for example, some of the bad things we do and how they boomerang:

- We say, "I've decided not to clean my room," and because we don't we find out we can't go out and play. Our decision boomerangs.
- We tell a lie about someone, and lo and behold it soon is voiced around that we told a lie. Our lie boomerangs.
- We claim we don't have to be kind, but then others in turn aren't very kind toward us. Our unkindness boomerangs.

Of course, the good we do may come back too:

- We help a friend, and then our friend gives us a helping hand when we need it. Our helpfulness boomerangs.
- We say an encouraging word about another person, who then is more likely to see good in us. Our encouragement boomerangs.
- We show love, and we are loved. Our love boomerangs.

So it goes. More often than not what we do comes right back to us. It's worth thinking about how our actions boomerang.

The Bible doesn't talk about boomerangs, but it does talk about how life boomerangs for us. Jesus said, "The measure you give will be the measure you get back."

Think about it.

Let us pray.

Dear God: May we remember that as we give, so we shall receive. Amen.

A Frisbee Lesson

Last week it was a boomerang. This week, it's—a Frisbee.

A Frisbee?

Did you ever think you'd see one of those coming out of my brown bag? I didn't, that is, not until late last Sunday. After we had talked about the boomerang I began thinking about the Frisbee. It seemed to me that there's something more to be said about the Frisbee than just how it's thrown or caught, or that it's a lot of fun.

How many of you have Frisbees? If you have one, raise your hand. Or if you don't have one but your older brother or sister does, or even if your dad or mom has one, raise your hand. Well, I'm not surprised.

Most everyone has a Frisbee. On a warm day, go to any park in our city and you'll see Frisbees flying here, there and yon. It's something both big and little people can do.

Even dogs. That's right, even dogs play with Frisbees. The other day I saw a man throwing one to his dog. As the Frisbee sailed through the air, and just before it fell to the ground, his dog would jump up and catch it in its teeth. Sometimes that dog would jump two or three feet off the ground. It was fun to watch.

And it's fun for us too. With that special flick of the wrist, the Frisbee is spinning across the playground, where in most instances someone tries to catch it before it hits the ground. Some even try to catch it in the funniest of ways, such as with one finger or between the legs or behind the back.

What makes a Frisbee fly?

A Frisbee flies, or rides, on a cushion of air. That's why it's shaped like this, with curved edges. When it's thrown correctly, flat (curved side down) and spinning, it traps the air underneath and sails along on a cushion of air. That cushion of air is an uplifting force.

So it is with us. No, we're not like a Frisbee in looks or shape or flying ability. But we are lifted up as we go through life.

I think of loving parents. Really loving parents, the kind you and I have, will do whatever they can to keep us from falling on the hard bumps of life. Their support is more than just a cushion of air. It's love that cares enough to lift us up and send us on life's way.

There are our friends. Good friends will say, "How can I help you?" Their support isn't just a lot of hot air, it's supporting love.

And of course there's God. Will God ever let us down? No. In the Bible it says, "The Lord lifts up" and "The wind of the Lord drives." This isn't about Frisbees, but it means that God wants to lift us and guide us as we sail through life. God really does love and care for us. Let's remember this the next time we throw a Frisbee.

Let us pray.

Dear God: Thank you for lifting and guiding us. Amen.

No. 22

Blow, Wind, Blow

It goes way back, back to when I was a child. In fact, it was one of the first toys I had. Yesterday, just as I was about to walk out of the store, there it was, and I couldn't resist buying it. It's in my brown bag.

Surely all of you have played with one of these—a pinwheel. All you have to do is hold it in the air and run, and this wheel goes around and around. The faster you run, the faster it goes. And if you don't want to run, then just move your arm around fast and it will go fast too. Or you can blow on it like this, and it spins.

As you can see, there's not that much to it. But it sure is fun. It was fun for me when I was young. And believe it or not, as old as I am now, it's still fun.

How many of you have a pinwheel? Good, I see a lot of you do.

For those of you who don't have one, I guess you could buy one. Or better yet, do what I learned to do as I got older. I made my own.

All you have to do is take an eight-inch square of paper that's fairly stiff (you don't want to use flimsy paper) and with a pair of scissors cut in from the four corners to an inch from the center. Then bring all the points into the middle and stick a pin through them and into a stick that's about two feet long.

That's it. You've made a pinwheel. If you forget how I said to do this, your parents will know how. They'll help you. Try it when you get home from church today.

I brought this pinwheel today because it makes me think of God.

"How," you're asking me, "could this funny-looking toy do that?"

Really, it's not the toy, it's the wind.

"But how is that," you may ask, "especially since you can't see the wind?"

That's just the point. No, we can't see wind, nor can we see God. I wish we could see God with our eyes just as we see one another. But that isn't what God wants us to do. Even in the Bible it says, "No one has ever seen God." When we talk about seeing God, what we're really talking about is knowing God in our hearts and minds. What God wants us to do is believe, for believing is a way of seeing.

Wind is a symbol. It is used to say something about something else, and here it says something about God.

I like the way wind is spoken of in the Bible. On a special day, called Pentecost, many of Jesus' followers came together in Jerusalem to talk about Jesus, who had just died, had been raised from death, and had gone to be with God. While there, they reported feeling the nearness of God, and they spoke of this as hearing the "rush of a mighty wind" (and at the time they were inside the house). This was their way of referring to God.

We can't see wind, but we can feel it flowing and pushing against us. So it is with God.

While we cannot see the wind, we can see what the wind does to the pinwheel. It moves it. It gets it going.

57

Isn't God trying to do the same with us? No, I don't feel any divine wind blowing in my face. While we can't see God, we can feel God moving us, getting us going. And my pinwheel reminds me about how God does this with you and me.

Let us pray.
Dear God: Just as we can feel the wind, may we also feel your presence. Amen.

No. 23

The Trinity

Have you ever seen a shamrock?
It's not a rock, it's a plant. And to show you what it looks like, I just happen to have one in my brown bag.

You've seen this kind of plant. And so have those who live in Ireland, that country across the ocean.

This is the official flower of Ireland. If you ever go to a St. Patrick's Day parade you'll see people wearing this little leaf in their lapels or pinned to their shirts. And on that day, a day to remember St. Patrick, people try to wear something green, the color of the shamrock, telling everyone that the wearing of the green is for the Irish.

There's a legend (a legend is a story of long ago which may or may not be true) that St. Patrick, a real man of the church who lived many years ago, planted the shamrock in Ireland because each leaf is shaped into three smaller parts. Did you notice that?

Let me pull off a leaf and show it to you up close. There. Isn't that pretty? See the three parts of the leaf? In fact, that's what the name shamrock means—three-leafed. You know, it looks like clover, the plant we sometimes find growing in our yards. But it's not the same.

According to the legend, St. Patrick planted the shamrock in Ireland, where he came to live and teach the people about God, because the leaves of these little

59

plants reminded him of the Trinity.

The Trinity? What's that? Do any of you know what is meant by the Trinity?

Let me say that this is a church word, and a very important one. Perhaps you've heard it used but didn't quite know what was meant by it. The Trinity is three ways of talking about God. These three ways are spoken of in the Bible (though the word Trinity isn't used there) as "of the Father and of the Son and of the Holy Spirit."

We often hear God spoken of as "Father." We could say "Mother" and mean the same, though back in the days when the Bible was written they used "Father." (This doesn't mean that God is either a male or a female.) By this we mean that God is that first great Parent, so to speak, who made the world and everything in it. This is just a way of talking about God, a way of speaking of God as the Creator.

The second part of the Trinity uses the word Son. This is about Jesus Christ. We believe that God has come to us in a very special way through this person named Jesus. Through him we are allowed to know more about God. And because Jesus is that special one, God's Son, who does this for us, we call him Christ. So when we talk about the second part of the Trinity, we find ourselves talking about God made known in and through Jesus Christ.

The third part of the Trinity is the Holy Spirit. Here we experience what those first followers of Jesus felt after he died. They sensed that God was still with them. They had known this when Jesus was alive, but now they began to realize that God's Spirit was just as near, if not nearer to them, as before. So they spoke of God in this way, the holy God with them still, the ever-present Spirit.

To this day we still talk about God in these three ways.

And the shamrock reminds us of this.

Let us pray.
Dear God: Thank you for letting us know you in these three special ways. Amen.

No. 24

For Fathers

I know you remembered! It's Father's Day.
Would any of you like to tell how you told, or showed, your father he's special?

Now it's my turn. My father lives far away from here. Because I was needed here this morning, it wasn't possible for me to go there to visit him on his day. I would have liked to have done that, for he is very special to me.

Over the years—and he has been my father for many years, more years than you might think—he has been a good father to me. When I had a question about something, or if I needed someone to listen to me talk about my hopes and dreams, or if I had a problem, or if I wanted a good golf game, he was always there. He still is, though I have to travel quite a distance to see him now.

As you can see, I feel close to my dad.

Since I wasn't able to go to where he lives, I telephoned him instead. Mainly what I said was that I loved him and that I wished him a happy Father's Day. I also hoped he would enjoy the gift I had sent him.

Speaking of a gift, I want to show you what my two children, Tap and Suzanne, gave me. As you know, I'm their father, their dad. Their gift to me is in my brown bag. While I get it out, I'd like you to close your eyes. Don't open them until I say to.

OK. How about this? It's an apron just for a dad who helps in the kitchen or who cooks over the backyard grill. I do both. What's printed on it is what gives me such a big smile.

OUR
DAD'S
THE
GREATEST

Isn't that a nice thing to say? It made me feel so proud, so happy. I hugged them both.

You may not have given your dad an apron like this, but that's not the point. The point is that whatever you gave him said the same thing. Your actions, your remembering, your attention—all say to this special man in your life, "You're the greatest!" And it would be nice if you were to say that to him—today.

That doesn't mean he's perfect, that he doesn't make mistakes. As a father—and I speak for all the fathers—I make my share of mistakes. We all do. Remember, we're human too. So keep that in mind and forgive whenever necessary.

But this shouldn't keep us from honoring our fathers. They are special, for they mean so much to us. One of the Ten Commandments (the fifth one) tells us to "Honor your father." Yes, let's give honor— meaning respect—where honor is due this day, to our fathers.

You know what? This makes God happy. Remember, it was God who said, "Honor your father."

Let's do it today, tomorrow, and every day.

Let us pray.
Dear God: Thank you for our fathers. Amen.

No. 25

Good Fortune to You

Last week my family and I went to a Chinese restaurant. We really enjoyed it. And at the end of our meal, we were served fortune cookies.

Do you know about fortune cookies? They are cookies that have little pieces of paper folded inside them, and on each piece of paper is a special message called a fortune. And what does the word fortune mean? It's something that may happen to you in the future. Here are some examples:

You will meet a forgotten friend.
What you want will happen next year.
You will receive something special soon.
You will live long in happiness and joy.

When I broke my cookie open, it read, "Good tidings will come shortly." That means I may soon hear something I will be happy to hear. What that will be, I don't know. But I like that fortune.

Fortune cookies are a favorite Chinese-American dessert. I have a friend who recently went to China, and she said she didn't see one fortune cookie there. Some people who should know say that fortune cookies were first made in the United States. Oh, well! No one remembers for sure who first made this kind of cookie. However, they first appeared in California a little over sixty years ago, about 1920, to advertise the opening of a Chinese restaurant. The idea caught on, and we've been eating them ever since.

That's what I want us to do this morning—eat some cookies with a fortune inside.

This past week my family and I became interested in making fortune cookies. We found a good recipe and directions in a magazine.* We made enough for us all. I would like to share them with you, so take one, but don't eat it before I tell you to. Just hold it.

Now break open your cookie. Before you eat it, look at the message in your cookie. I might add that the message in all these cookies is the same. Here's what it says: God "cares about you." That's from the Bible.

I put that message in our fortune cookies because that is the best message we could possibly receive. We're the most fortunate of people when we really believe this. We need to take this message very seriously.

Think about it. God cares about you and me, about each and every one of us. This means that in God we always have a friend. We can go to God with our troubles and our joys. God cares about you and me because God loves us. Never forget that.

You may eat your cookie. It's OK to eat it here. But then put this message of good fortune in your pocket and take it home with you. Read it over and over again until you know it by heart.

God cares about you.

Let us pray.
Dear God: Thank you for caring about us. Amen.

*"Fortune Cookies Unfold Their Secrets," *World,* vol. 42 (February 1979), pp. 19-21.

No. 26

Have a Longer Fuse

What important day is coming this week?
Fourth of July, of course.

And what do we do on that day besides eat, visit with family and friends, and celebrate our nation's birthday?

Shoot off fireworks, of course.

Speaking of fireworks, I would like to say a couple of things, and I want you to listen carefully. *This is very important.*

Fireworks are dangerous. I want to say that again, even louder. *Fireworks are dangerous.* They can hurt you. People have been injured very seriously when playing with fireworks. It happens every year. Some fireworks can even kill if they go off wrong. That makes them even more dangerous.

My advice is that you not use fireworks yourself. If

you already have them, let your parents shoot them off. It's even better to go to the park and watch the public fireworks. That's what our family does. The fireworks make a lot of noise and really light up the sky. It's a lot of fun—and it's safer.

In my brown bag, I have my own firecracker. Let me show you. It's safe, because I made it without any explosives. It's a big one. I'd say it's almost twelve inches long. Let's talk about my firecracker.

Have you ever heard the old saying about having a short fuse? This piece of white yarn is the fuse. If it is short and is lit, it's going to explode quickly.

That's the way we all are some of the time. We have a short fuse. We blow up quickly—meaning we get angry fast. Too fast. And what happens then is that we hurt not only ourselves but others as well. We need to have a longer fuse.

I've fixed my firecracker so this can happen. Watch me. By pulling on the fuse, it gets longer, longer, longer, and longer yet. Look at that—it's already two feet long.

In the Bible it says, "Let every [one] be quick to hear, slow to speak, slow to anger, for [our] anger . . . does not work the righteousness of God." That means that our anger keeps us from showing the love, the patience, and the understanding God wants us to show others.

So next time you start to get angry because of what someone has done or said to you, think about putting a long fuse on your feelings. Otherwise you might blow up too quickly, hurting not only yourself, but also someone else's feelings.

Yes, lengthen your anger fuse. Make it longer and longer and longer and longer.

Let us pray.
Dear God: Help us control our anger. Amen.

No. 27

Listening and Looking

When a fire truck goes clang, clang, clang
or
when a police siren goes uEEuEEuEEuEE
or
when an ambulance goes EEeeEEeeEEeeEEee
and
when their red lights are flashing, flashing, flashing, flashing what do you do?

Yes, that's what I do. I listen and look! Then I wonder what has happened.

I have in my brown bag this morning . . .

What do you think of that? A yellow hat, with a flashing red light on top and a siren. Here it goes . . .

You paid attention. You couldn't help yourself. I was sending out this signal, hoping you'd see and hear. And you did.

We all send out signals. Not this way, not with this kind of hat. But we often do it with the sound of our voices or in the look in our eyes or by how we act.

For example, when we talk louder and louder, even when we say that nothing is wrong, we are more than likely a little upset or excited.

Or when our eyes get as big as saucers, we're either surprised or frightened or both.

68

And when we begin to act in strange ways—like not behaving or being rather nervous or being very quiet—we may be sending a signal that something isn't right.

We need to learn how to listen for silent messages that tell us how others feel. But I especially want us to listen for those silent sirens that go off when people are hurting on the inside. Perhaps they are hurting for these reasons.

Someone said something to them or about them that they didn't like, that was unfair, unkind, unloving. And it hurt so much that all they felt like doing was crying—inside. But if we're listening to their silent messages, we know they feel bad on the inside. Then think what a welcome friend we'd be, and how good it would make them feel, if we were to say a kind word to them, put an arm around their shoulder, or perhaps give them a hug.

Or they may have lost a pet. Perhaps it ran away or even died. Or even worse, it could be the death of someone, like a grandparent or a friend, that has hurt them. Perhaps they don't know how to express in words how they feel, but their feelings show in their actions. Think how much better we feel when we know someone understands us at a time like this.

Or maybe they wanted something to happen and it didn't. Perhaps it was a baseball game lost or a friend who became unfriendly or a trip canceled. Just seeing the look on their faces tells us something is wrong, doesn't it? How wonderful it would be if we'd sense this kind of disappointment and let them know we understand.

We all have a way of telling, even without words, how others feel on the inside. Our happy feelings bubble over, and we can't keep quiet. It's those other feelings, those sadder ones, that are harder to put into words. There may be no loud siren or no flashing light, but the warning signals are there. Are we listening and looking? Do we care enough?

In the Bible it says, "Look not to your own interests, but also to the interests of others."

Let us pray.
Dear God: Help us to be more caring. Amen.

No. 28

It's Gone

"Now you see it, now you don't!"
That sounds like what a magician would say. With a puff of magic, a magician makes things disappear. A few nights ago I saw a magician make a rabbit disappear, and I'm still wondering how he did it. One minute the rabbit was in his hand, the next minute there wasn't anything in his hand. Gone. And his sleeves were rolled up. Where that rabbit went, I don't know. That's what the magician said: "Now you see it, now you don't."

Do any of you do magic? Can you make a rabbit disappear? I've always wanted to do that sort of thing, but I don't know how. However, in my brown bag I have something that's like magic. It's called a magic slate.

Here's how it works. With this plastic pencil, I can draw on this clear plastic sheet. Under it is another plastic sheet, which is light gray, and under all this is a black waxy backing. So when I draw—I'll draw a face, a happy face—the pencil makes a mark that presses the second sheet down into the black backing. Then— and here's what seems like magic—when I lift the plastic sheet away from the backing, the happy face disappears. Gone! Would you like to see that again?

By the way, with all magic tricks, no matter how difficult or puzzling, there is a way to explain what happened. How magic tricks are done isn't explained, and that makes us to wonder all the more. Just remember that there isn't any magic trick that can't be explained—somehow, some way. After all, the magician has to know how to do it.

With this magic slate, I want to explain something else. To do this, I'll draw another face, this time an unhappy face. Notice how the corners of the mouth turn down. Let's say this person has done something wrong, something bad, something that shouldn't have been done. We can understand what this means, for we've all been guilty of this, be it lying or taking something that didn't belong to us or being mean to someone else or not obeying Mom or Dad or . . . (the list of wrongs can be long at times). It doesn't mean that we do all these things, all the time, but we often do our share of what shouldn't be done. Right? And isn't this the way we look or feel, with both corners of our mouth turned down, when we're caught or questioned about the wrong we've done? Sure enough! So what are we to do about it?

If we were talking only about this drawing, all we'd have to do is lift the plastic sheet, like this, and the unhappy face would be gone. But if that is our own unhappy face, caused by the wrong we've done, it doesn't go away that easily. Magic won't do it.

Do you know the word forgiveness? Forgiveness is when one stops feeling angry toward someone who has done a wrong and says "It's OK now. This wrong will not be held against you anymore."

When a parent or friend or teacher says something like that to us, it takes away our unhappy face. Gone.

God wants to say that to us when we've done something wrong. God wants us to have a happy face. For that to happen, we need to say to God, "God, I'm sorry I did this wrong. Please forgive me." No, this isn't done with magic. It's done with God's love for us. We tell God we're sorry for what we've done and ask for forgiveness. God says in the Bible, "I will remember [your] sins and [your] misdeeds no more." Gone! That not only makes us happy, it also makes God happy.

Let us pray.
Dear God: Forgive us and then let your joy be in us. Amen.

No. 29

Like New

Are you afraid of snakes?
I understand. Some snakes are harmless,
others aren't. Just to be on the safe side, be careful.
Stay away from snakes.

If I told you I had a snake in my brown bag,
would you be afraid? Really, what I have isn't quite a
snake. Let me show you. Now, would I scare you? Not
me!

It's a snake skin.

This was found on my parent's farm. I'm not sure,
but I think this skin comes from a harmless kind of
snake. Have you ever seen a skin like this one?

A snake sheds its skin several times a year,
leaving it behind on the ground. You see, the new skin
has grown under the old one, so the old one isn't
needed anymore. Then the snake is like new, or at
least it has a new skin.

Did you know that we are continually in the
process of losing our skin? That's right. This isn't
happening all at once, as it did for this snake, but just
as the snake lost the old skin because new skin had
grown under the old, so it is with us. New skin is
always growing to take the place of the old. When we
bathe or shower, some of the old skin washes away. At
other times our skin gets dry and flakes off. Scientists
say that our skin, in fact every cell in our bodies, is
new every seven years. It's not something that happens
all at once, but over that period of time, we get all new
cells. Our skin is made up of many of those cells, and it

74

covers up our muscles and bones and the rest of our insides.

Does shedding our skin make us new people? If in a period of seven years, all our cells are made new (remember, cells are those little parts that make up the big parts of our bodies), then doesn't it stand to reason that we're new people after this has happened to us? Yes and no.

Our bodies, like our skin, are always becoming new. So in that sense, yes, we become new people. But aren't we still the same people we were before? We use the same names when referring to ourselves. Others still recognize us. But we are not quite the same. We'll change as we grow older, and we won't always act the same—it's hoped we'll act better. Still, we are us, aren't we?

Becoming a new person really has nothing to do with getting new skin or new cells. Rather, this happens when we change our ways.

God wants to help us to change, to be new. For this to happen, though, we need a new heart. I'm not talking about the heart that pumps blood throughout the body. Here we're talking about having a new desire to be better than we are. Before, we may have been unkind or unloving, thinking only of ourselves, sad, angry, hateful, or mean. If we have a new heart—which God wants to give us—then we'll be new people in how we act, more caring and loving, happier and more content. That's the most important thing that can happen to us. That's what God wants to do for us. And we have God's promise of this, written in the Bible: "A new heart I will give you, and a new spirit I will put within you." Then it happens: We become like new as God promises.

Let us pray.
Dear God: Make us new as you promised. Amen.

75

No. 30

Ever So Good

Last night before I went to bed I opened the refrigerator and took a good look. Surely my doing this didn't have anything to do with my diet. Or did it?

Have you ever gone without eating for a while, only to have your stomach tell you something?

Well, it was my stomach that wanted me to open the door of the fridge. And I saw many good things to eat, from meats to desserts. But I want to tell you right here in front of all these people that I didn't snitch any goodies. Oh, I looked at and longed for just a sample, but I kept hands off. *I'm still on a diet.*

I confess I did take one thing from the fridge, and I brown-bagged it this morning. It's one of my favorite foods, and perhaps yours too. Ketchup.

Don't you just love this stuff? I especially like it on french fries and hamburgers. What do you like it on?

By the way, I've heard it argued that ketchup isn't a food, that it's a "food helper"—whatever that means. Sure, it's not like meat and potatoes or even good vegetables. But to my way of thinking, it's sure good stuff, and it does help foods taste better.

That's one of the reasons I brought this bottle of ketchup. When I was looking in the fridge, this bottle caught my eye. Not having anything better to do, I took this ketchup bottle and read the label.

MADE FROM RED RIPE
TOMATOES, DISTILLED VINE-
GAR, CORN SWEETENER,
SALT, ONION POWDER,
SPICES, NATURAL FLAVORING.

After my trip to the refrigerator, I went to bed and
lay there thinking about this ketchup bottle and what it
said on the label. It occurred to me that what makes
ketchup so good, so helpful with other foods, are the
good ingredients (that's the stuff I read on the label)
that go into it. When the good goes in, the good comes
out.

Then I thought about you and me. We're good
too, and helpful to others, when good ingredients go
into us. Here I wasn't thinking about food, much less
ketchup. No, I was thinking about other good things,
such as:

love
    joy
        peace
            patience
                kindness
                    goodness
                        faithfulness
                          gentleness
                            self-control.

Think what we would be like with all these in us.
And with all of these in us, think how much good
would come out of us.

These so-called ingredients are found in the Bible,
and it was Paul who suggested we have them in us.
Here again is that list of good things we need within us
to make us ever so good. . . .

Let us pray.
Dear God: Fill us full with good stuff. Amen.

No. 31

More Than a Hobby

How many of you have a hobby? Perhaps you enjoy collecting stamps or dolls or baseball cards or rocks or autographs. Or maybe your hobby isn't collecting something but instead doing something, like swimming or playing a musical instrument or painting or fishing or building model ships. A hobby can be almost anything, because a hobby is something you enjoy enough that you'll spend a lot of your spare time doing it. So tell me, what's your hobby?

I too have a hobby. It started when I was just about your age. I collect arrowheads and other things Indians used in the olden days. Here's how I got started.

I lived on a farm in Oklahoma. That's a state where a lot of Indians lived, and still do. I didn't know much about the old-time Indians except what I saw in the movies on Saturday afternoon. One day I was looking out the kitchen window and I noticed a man in the field by the creek doing something odd. He would walk along, looking down, then every so often stop and bend over as if to pick something up. He was too far away for me to see what he was picking up. My first thought was that he was picking cotton, because he was in a cotton field. But he didn't have a cotton sack with him. Being curious, I went down to where he was, and (I can remember this so clearly) he showed me what he was doing—collecting arrowheads and other Indian objects. I walked along with him while he showed me what to look for, and ever since I've been looking and finding.

Let me show you some of the things I've found, which I have neatly tucked away in my brown bag. These are arrowheads. Indians tied the arrowheads to the end of arrows, and then the arrows were shot with a bow for hunting. As you can see, they come in all sizes. Here's a piece of Indian pottery, broken from a larger bowl. Look at these tiny beads that were sewn onto leather clothes and moccasins. This is a tomahawk, used when the Indians fought battles. And look at this, a pipe (broken before I found it).

At home I have some big stone bowls used for grinding grain.

As you can see, I like my hobby.

But there's something here I want to tell you that goes beyond my hobby. Look again at this tomahawk and this pipe.

We don't use tomahawks today, but we often have our anger ready to use. Maybe it's anger with a friend (or someone who was a friend) or with a brother or sister or with someone we don't like. We are often ready to get out our tomahawk of anger, so to speak, and go get 'em. Right? Wrong. We don't want to be tomahawk users.

Look at this pipe. I like to think of it as a peace pipe. The Indians often smoked a pipe together when they wanted peace and friendship, passing it from one person to another. The idea was that if they would sit down and smoke together, they would be friends and have no desire to fight.

Granted, we don't fight like Indians of old, but we can learn a lesson from them. I've seen a picture in a museum of hundreds of tomahawks buried in a deep hole. Apparently two warring tribes had decided to stop fighting, and we can imagine that they then smoked the peace pipe. We too can bury the tomahawk of anger and pass the pipe of peace. I'm not talking about a real tomahawk or a real pipe (and I'm not encouraging you to smoke a real pipe). I'm talking about getting along with one another—peacefully.

The great God we believe in will be pleased when we do this. Jesus said, "Blessed are the peacemakers, for they shall be called [children] of God."

Let us pray.
Dear God: We want to be your peacemakers. Amen.

No. 32

The Prize

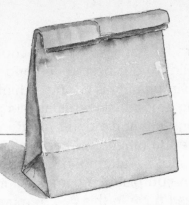

Normally I show you what's in my brown bag, but not this morning.

Don't look at me that way. Some of you look so disappointed, others look puzzled. I must insist on keeping my bag closed.

This afternoon is our church picnic. It's going to be held down at the park. Hope you're coming! We're going to have a lot of fun. Of course, there will be good food too. The weather looks great. Many games have been planned. That's the reason I'm not allowed to open my brown bag. You see, in here are the prizes for those games. Now you can understand why I'm keeping this bag tucked under my arm.

There are some good prizes in here. I know, because I helped select them. So come this afternoon, and maybe you'll win a . . .

It occurred to me that we all are prize-minded. We like to win. Winning makes us feel good. I can still remember prizes I won when I was your age and the good feeling I had then.

Did you know that even in the Bible prizes are mentioned? This is how it reads: "Do you not know that in a race all the runners compete, but only one receives the prize? So run that you may obtain it."

That means: Really try your best to win, for there is nothing wrong with winning.

The man who said this was Paul (I know you've

heard his name in church school). Yes, he said we should try our best to win and to win fair and square. To win unfairly is wrong. I think Paul would agree that being a good winner is also important. What this means is that we don't rub it in when we win and thus make the others feel bad or feel like losers.

So this afternoon when you run the races or when you play the games, all in an effort to win the prizes I have in this bag, remember to do your best. Agreed? Good.

But what if you don't win? Yes, you're to run, to compete, for the prize, the prize of doing the best you can. And what is the prize, even if you don't win? It's not in my bag. It's inside you. It is the good feeling you have when you know you've done your best. Never forget this, whether it be this afternoon at the picnic or tomorrow or whenever you are called on to compete. Others may at times do better, because they have more experience or because they have a lot of ability in a certain activity. But that shouldn't keep you from always trying your hardest, and even becoming better. When you do this, regardless of what others do, you're a winner—in an even more important way.

God wants us to do our best always. When we do our best, I'm sure God is pleased.

In the Bible, Paul also said, "I press on . . . for the prize of the upward call of God." You see, God is calling us to do our best—not our second best, but our best—whether we win or lose. And this goes for every good thing we do.

Let us pray.
Dear God: To you we give our best. Amen.

No. 33

A Fish Story

Want to go fishing?
How many of you have gone fishing? Did you catch any?

We just came back from a vacation high in the Rocky Mountains. We fished in a beautiful little lake. We caught a lot of fish, and we ate a lot.

I brought a fish back from our trip, and it's in my brown bag. No, it doesn't smell. You can't smell this fish anymore. Maybe it smelled forty-five million years ago. What did I say? Forty-five million years ago? That's right. And here it is.

This is a fossilized fish. It's called a *Diplomystus humilus*. That's some name, isn't it? No, I didn't catch it. I bought it in a store in Ouray, Colorado. I couldn't catch this kind of fish, for it lived millions of years ago. But, it was caught in a special way.

You see, something happened millions of years ago. The lake this fish was swimming in filled up with a lot of mud. This little fish, plus many more, was trapped in the mud and died. As time went by, the mud turned to rock. When this piece of rock was found and broken open, there inside was the imprint of this fish. Whoever found it sold it to the store that in turn sold it to me. And here it is. How's that for a fish story? And it's true too.

Looking at this fossil, I become excited. Just thinking of how old this little fish is makes me wonder all the more about what it must have been like then. If I had lived then and caught this fish, would it have tasted good? Maybe not. It's kind of small. In the store where I bought it, there's a bigger fossil that shows the imprint of a fish that must have weighed about fifteen pounds. And you should have seen the teeth it had! But that fossil, and the others I saw, made me wonder what the world was like so long ago.

I wonder about more too. I believe that this old fish, and those we caught last week in that beautiful lake, were all made by God. In the very first chapter of the Bible we read, "In the beginning God created. . . ." Since that is so, then all living things, living now or in the past, were made by God. How else could it be, since God is the great Creator? And in that first chapter of the Bible it says further, "And God said, 'Let the waters bring forth swarms of living creatures.'" Well, this little fish was one of those millions upon millions of living creatures.

And it says in the Bible, "And God saw that it was good."

You know, we have a great God. From the world's beginnings, which the scientists tell us was a lot longer ago than when this fossil fish lived, God has been creating, always bringing new life to live on this earth. The fish we caught on our trip would not have been in that lake if it hadn't been for God's making fish in the first place. And come to think of it, I guess we wouldn't be here either if it weren't for God.

We're alive. We're not old fossils like this fish. So let's give God our thanks for all living things.

Let us pray.
Dear God: Thank you for all you have created and all you are creating. Amen.

84

No. 34

Our Cornerstone

What is a cornerstone?
A cornerstone is a special stone placed in the corner of the foundation when a building is being built. A cornerstone usually has something special written on it, like the date the building is being built, the name of the building, or the name of the builders. Almost always it is put in place when a lot of people are present, when some speeches are made about the importance of the new building.

Often special things are put inside the stone. You see, a hole is cut into it, on the back side, and a metal box is put in there. Newspapers, pictures, important bits of information, and other items of interest are put into the box. This is done so that many years later, if the cornerstone is ever taken out and the box is opened, the people then can learn what it was like when the building was built.

Did you know that our church has a cornerstone?

After church this morning, if you'd like to see it, meet me at the front door and I'll show it to you.

When they put our cornerstone in place, when they were beginning to build this church (which is now almost a hundred years ago), the members put some things into the cornerstone. They put
- copies of the city papers (printed that day)
- a map of the city
- a list of the church members

- drawings of how they wanted the church to look
- and, to mention one more (oh, there really are too many other things to mention them all now), the names of all the children who helped raise money for the new church.

By the way, we know how much money the children earned. Just before the cornerstone was put in place the clay jugs containing money were broken and the money was counted. They didn't put the money inside the cornerstone, but they did record the amount on a slip of paper: $78.26.

Would you like to see the cornerstone—now? I have it in my brown bag. What? No, I don't have the actual stone, I have a rubbing of it. And here it is.

What I did was tape a piece of paper over the cornerstone and rub it with the side of a crayon. It's called a stone rubbing.

While I was doing this I couldn't help but wonder if the church is rubbing off on us. By this I mean:
- We talk about God here, but do we talk about God when we're not here?
- Jesus was loving and kind, and asked us to be the same way, but are we?
- The Bible is read here, but do we read it at home?
- Being a good person, being honest, being caring, being helpful are some things we talk a lot about here, but is that what we're like at school or at home?

Is what we're saying and doing here rubbing off on us? Put another way, is it having any effect on us?

It's one thing to put all this in our thoughts and seal it up like the things they put inside this cornerstone. But it's something else to let our religion show in ways that make a difference in our lives, every day.

Notice. On the outside of our cornerstone are two

things. First, there's a cross. Second, there are some words written in another language (Latin)—"*Nil Sine Numine.*" That means "Nothing without divine aid." And this means for us that we're a Christian church and we can't do without God's help. May that be the thought that rubs off on us here, so that when we are not here it really makes a difference in our lives. Let us live what we learn here about God's will for us.

Let us pray.
Dear God: May your will and help through Jesus Christ rub off on us. Amen.

No. 35

Mirror, Mirror

I must be very careful with what I have in my brown bag. I don't want to break it.

It's a mirror. Look into it, and tell me what you see.

Now, I'll take a look and tell you what I see. I don't see you, I see me. But when you looked you saw you instead of me. That's the way a mirror is supposed to work. It's to reflect, or let you see, the person who is looking into it.

The thing I notice—if you and I look at the same time—is that we're different from one another.

Wait a minute. In many ways we're alike. We each have eyes, ears, a nose, a mouth, and hair. Yes, in so many ways we're alike.

But if we could all look together into this mirror, and if we looked closely, we'd note that we're really not alike. We are all different.

That's the way God wants it to be. Just like snowflakes, no two of us are exactly alike.

Some of the differences can be seen clearly, for some of us are short, some medium, some tall, and some extra tall. Some are skinny and some are not so skinny. Some have short hair and others wear their hair long.

Speaking of hair, it comes in many different colors, such as brown, black, blonde, red, and white.

As for skin color, there's brown, black, yellow, red, and white.

Yes, we're all different, and that's the way God

wants it.

But that isn't always the way we want it, is it? Sure, we do want to be different up to a point, But how many times have we said that we want to be like others?

We hear ourselves saying, "Susan and Tommy have that new kind of jeans, the ones with the special design on the hip pocket, and I want a pair like that so I can look like them."

Or we hear, "Where did you get your hair cut, for I'm going to get mine cut just like yours."

Or again, "If only I were as good-looking, as smart, as you are!"

There's nothing wrong in comparing ourselves. But beware. God doesn't want you to be that other person. God wants you to be you, not someone else. Why? Because God made you special.

How often we hear ourselves saying, "I don't like the way I am. I wish I were someone else."

No, God would rather hear each of us say, "I am who I am, and God made me who I am," and then go on to say, "If I need to change for the better, let that happen to me, but I still want to be me."

Paul in the Bible wrote this: "I wish that all were as I myself am." What do you think of that? To him we need to say, "No, we don't want to be like you, we want to be us—not you!" Even Paul understood the importance of this, for he went on to say, "But each has his [or her] own special gift from God, one of one kind and one of another." And this gift is that we are each different and special.

Whenever you look into a mirror, remember to see the you God sees—you!

Let us pray.

Dear God: Thank you for making each of us special. Amen.

No. 36

Stretch It

As all of you know, I bring many things to church in my brown bag. And each Sunday, even before church starts, some of you ask me what's in here, and I always say, "Just you wait and see!" From worms to sandpaper, from the comics to the Bible, from plants to rocks—you name it and it has been in here for me to take out and talk about. If it hasn't been in here, it will be before long—just wait and see.

I was thinking about this the other day as I was looking in my desk drawer. From that drawer have come pencils, paper clips, erasers, string, a ruler, and many other things. Today out of my desk drawer comes something you've seen many times. A rubber band.

What are rubber bands for?

To keep things bundled together.

I know what some of you are thinking, or at least this is what I think some of you are thinking: Rubber bands are for shooting spit wads or for flicking someone. Right?

Wrong. That's a misuse of the rubber band. The main purpose is to keep things bundled together.

But there is another use for the rubber band, and I want us to think about it this morning. Notice how it stretches. Its stretching reminds us of something we need to think about every day. Maybe this is why I'm so fond of the rubber band, because it makes me think of stretching. We need to stretch too.

For example, we need to stretch our bodies with

good exercise. God has given us our bodies, and it's important that we take good care of them. If we don't exercise, like running, jumping, or walking, we get flabby muscles and become weak. But even worse, we tend to be more sickly, and the older we become without exercising, the more likely we are to have serious health problems. So we need to keep active. That's really a way of giving thanks to God for our bodies. So stretch . . .

We need to stretch our minds too. God wants us to think, to use our minds. God has given us the ability to reason, to remember, to wonder, to reflect, to study, to question, to use our brains. And since God wants us to think, to use our brains, we need to learn to do this the best we can. This too is a way of giving thanks to God.

Again, we need to stretch our love. Do we love enough? I think we can all talk to ourselves about this. We can all think of someone—maybe a brother or a sister or a friend—we don't love as we should. And while saying this, we're reminded again of the lesson of love we've learned here, as Jesus taught: Love when loving isn't easy. Let's stretch that way too.

And we need to stretch our faith—believe more in God. Does this mean knowing more about God? No, we don't know everything about God. It's important, though, to know as much as we can, as much as God allows us to know. But God is so great, and we're so small, that it's impossible to know all about God. Faith means having more trust in God. God can be trusted, completely and fully, and we know this because God loves us. Let's stretch our faith around that love.

For each of you I have a rubber band to remind you to keep stretching.

Let us pray.
Dear God: Help us as we try to do this. Amen.

No. 37

The DUO Club

How many of you belong to a club? What kind is it?

Want to join another one?

"What club?" you ask.

It's called the DUO Club. What? You haven't heard about it? Well, how could you, especially since we're starting it only this morning. You can join now— if you want to.

Maybe I'd better tell you what this club is about. The letters *D-U-O* stand for "Do Unto Others." Have you ever heard that before? Sure you have. It comes from the Bible: "As you wish that [people]would do to you, do so to them." Jesus said that. Now, the way we often say it is like this: "Do unto others as you would have others do unto you." Jesus said that. It's called the Golden Rule. And that is what I want us to do. Another way of saying this is to say, "Treat others as you want to be treated."

Makes sense, doesn't it? As least it does to me. It is certainly the fair thing to do. If I want to be fairly treated, then others around me want to be fairly treated too. If I ask them to do this for me, it's only right that I treat them the same way.

So before joining, let's go over the rules.

Rule One: Put yourself in the other person's place.

For example, if your sister isn't feeling well and loud noises make her feel worse, lower your voice and walk quietly, for you would want her to do the same for you if you were sick. Or if your brother has gotten into trouble, don't add to his problems by teasing him about it, for you wouldn't want him to tease you about your troubles. Again, when you ask for help and Mom and Dad give it, it's only fair to help them when they ask, for think how they would feel if you only took but didn't give.

Any questions?

Rule Two: Each day double check to see if you are doing Rule One.

Before you go to bed would be the best time to do this. Look back over the day's DUO Club activities and ask yourself if you've been a good club member by treating others as you would want to be treated. Think about each person you've dealt with during that day and ask yourself if that is the way you would like to have been treated. Be honest.

Any questions?

Rule Three: Ask for forgiveness when you've failed.

When you say your prayers, after recalling how you've treated others that day, ask God to forgive you if you have not treated someone well. Then ask God to help you be a better DUO Club member tomorrow.

Any questions?

Rule Four: Try again tomorrow.

Remember, we can be better than we are, and if we fail today we can make it right tomorrow.

Any questions?

Want to join?

No one is being forced to join this club. It's strictly voluntary—it's up to you. For all who want to join, I have a membership badge in my brown bag. It's for you to wear, beginning now. On the back is some masking tape that will help stick it on. You don't have to wear it all the time. But put it up somewhere in your room so that you can see it each day to remind you that you now belong to the DUO Club of our church.

Let us pray.
Dear God: Help us to be good members of the DUO Club. Amen.

No. 38

Controlling Our Temps

If you don't mind, I'm going to check my temperature. In my brown bag I have a thermometer.

Mmm mm, mmmmmm mmmm.

Wait a minute. You can't understand me with this in my mouth. Besides, I'm not supposed to talk when my temperature is being checked. And since I've already sat down to talk with you, I had better wait until later to take my temperature.

I feel OK. No fever. Tell me the truth—I look OK, don't I? The way I look is the way I feel. Perhaps someone will say, "Well, then, he must feel pretty bad!"

When was the last time you held a thermometer in your mouth? Were you sick? Did you have to go to bed? Do you remember what your temperature was? Remember, 98.6 is considered normal. This may go either up or down, and still be normal, depending on the person. The other day I was at the hospital to donate blood, and they took my temperature. It was 97.5.

By the way, when they took my "temp" (that's what they call it at the hospital), they didn't use a thermometer like this. Instead they put a thing in my mouth that looked like a white plastic ballpoint pen. Attached to it was a rubber tube connected to a metal box. On the face of the box were numbers that lit up. I sat there and watched as it showed my temp.

The way we usually take our temperature is with a thermometer we call the "mercury-in-glass" type, invented several hundred years ago by a Mr.

Fahrenheit. It's a tube of glass with a hole in the middle of it, closed at the top with a bulb of mercury at the bottom. (This silvery stuff is the mercury.) Along the sides are numbers. When the mercury warms up, it expands, meaning it takes up more space than before. Then it moves up the tube, measuring the user's body warmth.

Looking at this thermometer makes me think of those times when I've warmed up and I wasn't sick—the times I became angry and my temper flared. Oh, yes. That's happened to me, more times than I like to admit. Usually, after my temper has gone up, I say a few unpleasant things to the person who made me angry. Then I feel bad.

You know what I mean. Temper can make us feel bad—and I'm not talking about being sick. Why do we feel bad? Because we know that our quick temper can hurt others.

Although we are taught in church to love others, there is a right time and reason to get angry with someone, as well as a right way to let that person know how we feel. It's OK to tell someone we're angry. If we bottle up our emotions by not telling how we feel, this isn't good for us. But temper is different. It needs to be controlled. When our temper goes up, are we checking it?

In the Bible it says, "A man of quick temper acts foolishly." And again, "He who has a hasty temper exalts folly." What this means is that if we let our temper control us or speak for us, we may say the wrong thing or do the wrong thing, and that will hurt.

So let's check our temperature—temper wise—to control it before it goes too high. With God's help we can do this, and do something about it.

Let us pray.
Dear God: Help us to control our temper. Amen.

No. 39

Hear and Understand

I would like to introduce a friend: Mr. Dave Seyfert. If he were smaller, I would have put him in my brown bag and popped him out just about now.

Speaking of my brown bag, that's why I've invited Dave to sit with me this morning. First let me show you the bag (it's from a local supermarket), then I'll explain its connection with him.

Notice there's nothing in the bag. It's what's printed on the outside that's important: the alphabet for deaf people. Deaf people can't hear. One of the ways they talk is with their hands. These hand pictures (or I should say pictures of hands held in different positions) help them to talk in a special way.

Can any of you sign the alphabet with your hands? Dave, show us how this is done and sound out each letter as you do it.

Since deaf people can't hear, this is the way they talk—with their hands. When they want to say just one word, they finger-spell, using the alphabet on this bag. But since that would take a long time to spell out every letter of every word, they can talk with their hands to say what they want in a quicker way. When they move their hands and arms in certain ways, they can say a lot more. Each movement has a meaning.

Dave, let's show the children how that works. With my voice I'll say the words, and you say the same in sign language. Let's sign the Lord's Prayer.

Our Father, who art in heaven,
  hallowed be thy name.

Thy kingdom come,
Thy will be done,
    on earth as it is in heaven.
Give us this day our daily bread.
And forgive us our debts,
    as we forgive our debtors.
And lead us not into temptation,
    but deliver us from evil.
For thine is the kingdom,
    and the power,
    and the glory,
    forever. Amen.

Do you know what I noticed when Dave was signing the Lord's Prayer with his hands? Each and every one of you was paying extra special attention. Now, if I hadn't said the words along with him, you wouldn't have known what he was saying. But you would have watched his every move, knowing that he was saying something to you.

Well, we're not deaf, but too often we act as if we are, meaning that we don't listen to what others are saying to us. That's sad, for often they are telling us something we need to hear. Maybe it's our parents talking, or maybe our teacher at school or our teacher in church school, or maybe it's someone else we need to listen to.

Paying extra special attention is what it's all about. We certainly become better when we hear what we need to hear—and change for the better. So say to yourself: When someone is speaking to me, I'll listen carefully and try my best to understand.

And let's do the same when we hear God speaking to us through others.

In the Bible it says, "Hear and understand."

Let us pray.

Dear God: Help us to hear and understand. Amen.

No. 40

Ring That Bell

I want to tell you something about this church.
When you stand outside and look up at it, you see a bell tower, a belfry.

When you go home today, take a look. Then look again, and notice that there's no bell in the bell tower. Why not? Let me tell you that interesting story.

Years ago, when they built this church (a very long time ago, back in 1889) there was a city rule that big bells and loud whistles were not to sound because there were people who had come to this town to get well. You see, in the early years of Colorado Springs, hundreds and hundreds of people came here because they had tuberculosis, a very serious disease of the lungs. This was an ideal place because of the sun and dry air for these sick people to live while they got better. (This was before they had good medicine for that disease.) To keep from waking these sick people who needed rest, the city wouldn't allow the bells or whistles to sound at certain times. Sunday morning was one of those times, and since that is when the church people would most want to ring our bell, they just never got a bell. This is the story I've been told.

I hope we can get a bell. Times have changed, and now people with tuberculosis don't come here as they used to. Because of good medicine, they can stay where they live and be treated.

Have you ever thought about a bell? In my brown

99

bag I have one. This isn't the kind of bell we'd want to put in the belfry, is it? It's too small.

And what kind of bell is this? It's called a cowbell. This particular bell comes from the country of Switzerland, where they put this kind of bell around the necks of cows so they can hear where the cows are even when they can't see them. Makes sense. How do you like the sound of it?

Have you ever thought what a bell would be like if the tongue of the bell—that's the little ringer piece on the inside of it—were taken out, or never put in in the first place? There wouldn't be any sound. What's good about a bell that doesn't ring out? Nothing, I'd say.

When we come to church, we're supposed to learn how to make good sounds for others to hear. Just as a bell is to sound forth, so are we. How? By telling what we believe about God, Jesus, love, life, and many other important things.

But what if we were to keep quiet? No one would hear us, and they wouldn't know the good news we know.

When you go to your church school class, you're not going to be a bell, that I know. But you're going to learn to sound forth in a way that will make others say, "Isn't that good to hear? I want to hear more."

Sound out what's important to hear: let it be heard. Tell others about God and Jesus. Ring out the good news.

Let us pray.

Dear God: Like bells, help us to give a good, happy sound for others to hear. Amen.

No. 41

We're Worldwide

I'm a real cut-up. That's why I have a piece of paper and a pair of scissors in my brown bag. See?

Notice how I've folded the paper. It's been folded back and forth as many times as possible. This is called an accordion fold. Then I folded that in half from top to bottom.

Let me begin cutting.

As I do this, I want to remind you that today is a very special day. What's so special about this first Sunday in October? If this were Christmas or Easter or even Thanksgiving, there would be no question about this being a special day. But in October? Is this just an ordinary Sunday? No.

By the way, there is no such thing as just an ordinary Sunday. Every Sunday is special—or at least it should be. Why? Because we go to church and talk about God, pray to God, and feel God's nearness. When we do that, it's a special day.

I'm finished. I've done all the cutting I need to. With all these scraps of paper, I guess I should have brought a wastebasket. Ah, I'll use my brown bag as a wastebasket.

Let me show you what we have when I unfold the paper—people, all holding hands.

In my brown bag I also have a globe. On it I'm going to tape these people holding hands. There.

What's so special about this day? With these

paper people and this globe, I want to answer that question.

This day is called World Communion Sunday, a day when we and other Christians around the world take communion and in so doing say something important—that we all belong together, all members of the church worldwide.

As you perhaps know, there are many different church groups, like Methodist, Baptist, Lutheran, Presbyterian, and United Church of Christ, plus there are Roman Catholics and Eastern Orthodox. That's just a few of the groups there are in the larger church. Maybe it would help to think of it like this: There are many families in our church here, and although we're all different, we all belong together as the church. Well, all these church groups—all around the world—are different in many ways, yet despite their differences they belong together as the Christian church. Jesus has called us *all* to be the church, each in our own way, carrying on the work he started long ago.

Today Christians all around the world are taking communion, just as we're doing here. Together we're the church. It's like holding hands all around the world as Christ's people—the Christian church worldwide.

Let us pray.

Dear God: It's good to know there are Christians all around the world. Amen.

No. 42

Oh, So Beautiful!

It's that time of year again. To prove it, I have something for each of you in my brown bag. Let me pour them out so it will be easier for you to take one. They're aspen leaves.

This is the week when the aspens are prettiest, when they are changing their colors. All summer long these leaves were green, but now, as you can see, they are golden yellow. Some have just a bit of orange in them. When I look at these leaves, all I can say is "Beautiful."

I've been told these beautiful colors are in the leaves all summer and we just couldn't see them. The green hid the colors. It's only when the green fades away that we see the yellows and oranges—tinged with red. The beauty was there all along and we couldn't see it.

Yesterday my family and I went for a drive to see the aspen, up around Cripple Creek and Victor. Surely, you've been up to those two towns on the other side of Pikes Peak. I hope you and your family get a chance to go up and see the aspen this year. It's a beautiful drive. The mountains are covered with all these wonderful colors.

As I was driving home, it occurred to me that it would be nice to bring you a little bit of this color. So I've brought you these leaves. Please, each take one.

What God makes is beautiful, like the aspen, but also the mountains, the blue sky, the rolling countryside, the streams, and on and on. Do we take time to look and say "Beautiful!" and then to tell God how much we love this world made for us?

As I was driving home, it also occurred to me how important it is to look for beauty in the world—and not just in the leaves or in rocks or in the sky, but also in the lives of people.

How do we see this? We see it in a smile, a kind word, a good deed, a helping hand, a caring touch, a big hug. Are we looking for that kind of beauty—in others? It's there. And are we telling God how much we love this kind of beauty when we see it?

When others are looking for beauty, and when they look in our direction, do they see it in our lives? Or are we hiding it from them with actions that aren't beautiful?

Yes, there's a lot of beauty in God's world. Let's be part of it by letting it show in our lives by the way we love others.

And when you look at your beautiful leaf, think about the beauty you can show—with love.

Let us pray.

Dear God: For all that is beautiful, we give you thanks. Amen.

No. 43

The Promise of Tomorrow

Winter is almost here. You know that. The weather has begun to change. Oh, we're still having a few nice days, but it's been cold enough to wear heavy coats, especially early in the morning or late at night. There has been frost on the pumpkins and on car windshields and on flowers.

Speaking of flowers, this has been my summer! Never have I had such good luck growing flowers, and never were they so beautiful. There were many, many different kinds, and so many colors. Maybe it was because we had lots of rain, but I like to think it was my efforts, my ability, to grow flowers, that did it. However it happened—and I give God most of the credit—it sure was something to behold. We took pictures of the yard, back and front, and sent them to family members who were no doubt surprised. We sent them many pictures, taken from every angle. Now I look forward to next summer and growing more flowers.

Yesterday I was looking at some of the old flower plants, dead and shriveled up. That's what the weather does to flowers when the temperature gets below freezing. I went out to look, because on my day off I need to clean out the old flower plants and make the flower beds neater looking. As I do that tomorrow, you can imagine I'll be thinking about next summer.

But here's something else worth thinking about. In

my brown bag I have a clear plastic bag, and in it are some dried-up flowers. That's what an old dried up flower looks like. This is a marigold. Not much to look at, is it? When I take out all the dried up flower plants in my garden, I'm first going to snip off the old, dead flowers. Would anyone care to guess why?

Here's why. Watch. When I take this out of the plastic bag very carefully, and then rub it in my hands, note what happens. At first glance it looks just like a dead flower crumbled up. It is, but there's more. Look again. Among the crumbled-up parts of the dried flower are seeds. Flower seeds are for planting, and I'm going to save these until next spring and plant them then. Good idea—if I do say so myself.

But here's an even better idea. This is God's way of preparing for the future. God is always preparing for what is to come. Isn't that wonderful?

Yes, flowers will fade and shrivel up. They do that every year when they're through growing, when at last they die. It's as it says in the Bible, "The flower fades; but . . ."

However, listen to what else is said in this biblical passage: ". . . but the word of our God will stand for ever." I take this to mean that God's promise will not fade, as the flower does when its life is over. Rather, because God is ever looking ahead, so can we. With God we have the promise of tomorrow, for God is even now planning ahead.

Let us pray.
Dear God: For the hope you give us, we thank you. Amen.

No. 44

Roots

We're 107 years old today.
Of course, I'm not talking about you and me. We're not that old, are we? Tell me, please, that I don't look that old.

But our church is. Today is our anniversary Sunday, that special day when we recall how old we are. Like any birthday, we have a cake to eat after the worship service. My mouth is already waiting for it, and I know yours is too.

Yesterday I put on my old clothes and went down to the creek not far from where I live. There I looked and looked until I found what I wanted to bring this special morning. I've got it in my brown bag.

It's a root, a rather long root.

Let me tell you about roots. Roots help plants grow. They give life to the plant on top of the ground. If there weren't any roots, the plants could not live, for they couldn't get any water or food (plant food, that is) from the soil. Yes, aside from keeping the plant stationed in the ground so the wind won't blow it away, the roots help keep the plant alive. This plant—I'm not sure exactly what kind of plant it is—has a very deep root system.

This long root makes me think of our church. Our church has a very deep root system. Our roots may not go into the ground, but they go back into the past—back 107 years. What happened over the past 107 years has helped give us life today. We often forget this when we're so busy with what's happening today and planning for the future. But it's important for us to remember what has been done in this church over the past 107 years. What happened then still affects us today, in more ways than we realize. We need to learn and to recall our history—and a special history it is. That's what we're doing this morning.

But our roots go deeper yet, for our history as a church is more than just 107 years. We're really almost two thousand years old. Wow! You see, we go all the way back to Jesus. That's when the Christian church was started. No, not this local church on this corner in Colorado Springs. The first members here came from other churches started by Christians before them. This goes back and back and back to the early days when Jesus and his disciples started the church. Yes, our roots go deep into the church's history, to the very beginning.

Any questions?

Do you know who allows the church to grow—if we may speak of the church as a plant, and a wonderful plant it is? God, that's who. God wanted the church to grow, to bloom. And it has, in us here as well as in churches around the world. It says in the Bible, "God . . . gives the growth." That's why our church continues to live. God wants the church here and everywhere to grow and grow and grow. Many years from now the members of this church will speak of us as part of this church's root system that gave life to it while we worked here and worshiped here.

Let us pray.

Dear God: For the roots of this our church, and for the life our church has today, we thank you. Amen.

No. 45

A Mighty Pull

Have I something to show you!
But before I do, I want to ask if you know about magnets. You do? Good.

Isn't it strange how they work? A magnet will pull certain kinds of metal to itself. For example, I just happen to have in my brown bag a small magnet and some paper clips. Look how the clips are drawn to this magnet. It looks like they are stuck to it. Isn't that interesting?

Let's look again inside my brown bag. And wouldn't you know, I have a very big magnet, one of the biggest I've ever seen that could be held by hand. This one weighs about five pounds, or maybe a bit more. A friend lent it to me. He thinks it came out of a big motor, the kind used on large ships or in large factories.

Anyway, it's certainly the largest magnet I've ever played with. And does it have a powerful pull. Here are some pieces of metal. Just to show you . . . WOW! Did you see that? That piece of metal seemed to jump to the magnet. Let's see it again. Notice how much pulling it takes to get the piece of metal off the magnet. Again. WOW!

Just to show you how much of a pull this big horseshoe-shaped magnet has, I'm going to ask Aimee to pull it off. You can use both hands if you want to. In fact, I think you'll need to use both. You did it! But it didn't want to let loose, did it? Tim, do you want to try? OK, give it a tug. And you did it too! But it wasn't as easy as you thought. That's some magnet!

It's not my intention to make this a science class. I know magnets are used to produce electricity and that telephones, televisions, and radios wouldn't work without one of these—though not as big as this one. Also, I know that the earth, in its own way, acts like a great big magnet (which in turn makes a compass work). There's a lot I don't know, but this I do know. A magnet works. But this special hunk of metal also says something else to me. It's pulling power causes me to think of—God!

Just so you don't get a mistaken idea, or think I'm funny, no, I'm not saying God either looks like this big magnet or works the same way. That would be foolish. What makes me think of God, however, is that we are always being pulled, or drawn, toward God.

I like the way a man by the name of Augustine, who lived hundreds of years ago, spoke of this (and I have to say this is one of my favorite sayings), "Thou hast made us for thyself, and our hearts are restless until they find their rest in thee." That means God has made us so that we are truly happy only when we're close to God. Until that happens, we're not really happy on the inside.

Now can you see why a magnet, especially this big one, makes me think of God?

We can feel God's pulling power on our lives. I believe that this is one of the main reasons we've come here this morning, because God is even now causing us to want to know more about, and be nearer to, God. We're being attracted to this powerful pull on our

110

lives. The closer we get, the more we are drawn closer. Of this it says in the Bible, "Draw near to God and [God] will draw near to you." Then God's pull can hold us forever.

Let us pray.
Dear God: Have your powerful way with us. Amen.

No. 46

I Don't Want to, But

It's something I need to do every day, and I don't really enjoy doing it.

Do you have some things which you need to do, but if you're really honest about how you feel, you don't want to do them? Before I tell you what I'm referring to as my "have-tos-but-don't-want-tos," you tell me some of your "have-tos-but-don't-want-tos."

Now, let me tell you what I have to do every morning, even though I don't want to. In fact, I have my problem in my brown bag. It's my razor. I have to shave every morning, and it's a real drag.

There was a time, before I started growing hair on my face, that I thought it would be fun to shave. I said to myself, "It must be a lot of fun to be grown up." I couldn't wait for this to happen, but now I wish I could forget about it.

Don't get me wrong, for I have nothing against a bushy beard—on someone else. If someone wants to grow a beard, if he wants the joy of not shaving, I say "Go for it!" I would like the joy, but not the beard. It's just that I like a smooth, shaven face on me. So each morning I do this (*strokes*) with my razor, hoping I don't do this—"Gotcha ya!" (That's when I cut myself.)

When I shave, I look in the mirror—which isn't the best picture that early in the morning—and I talk to myself. One of the things I say to myself is that shaving is something I need to do because it's important. My dislike for doing it is beside the point.

That's the way it is. One of the words we use to talk about this is duty.

We all have duties. For example, you may not enjoy doing your homework, especially when your friends are asking you to come out and play. But you know that if you don't do your homework, you won't learn as much as you should.

And we all have a duty to be truthful. In the Bible we learn about the importance of telling the truth. We may wish we could tell it another way, a way that would make us seem better than we are. But we have a duty to tell it as it is, even if it hurts or makes us squirm.

Also, there is a need to be more loving, even to those who aren't very loving. It's our duty. Jesus said, "This I command you, to love one another." We may not want to love a particular person, but . . .

Every day there are things we all have to do, for the simple reason that we need to—it's the right thing to do. To do them is important, and it helps others as well as ourselves.

My advice is to talk to yourself each morning—and you don't have to do this as you shave—about doing the duties you have to do, to get on with them, and to finish them. Then see if you can find joy in what you do. Yes, when you finish what you need to do, there is joy awaiting you. I know, for I've experienced that joy myself.

Let us pray.
Dear God: Help us do our duty. Amen.

No. 47

A Piggy Bank

Do you get an allowance?
Do you save it, or spend it?

I'm not going to ask how you spend it. That could be any way—for this or that, or for that or this. The world offers us all kinds of ways to spend our money, some wise, some foolish. I've done both. We all have.

How do you save your money?

I hope you save some of it. If you were to spend it all, think how sad you'd be when you found something you wanted to buy and didn't have enough money to buy it. If you have that little extra put aside—saved—and it seems wise to spend it on what you want, think how happy that will make you. That's possible only if you save some money.

I have a piggy bank. Where? In my brown bag, of course. And this piggy is just oinking to get out.

How many of you have a piggy bank?

Does this look like Miss Piggy? No, this piggy isn't that good-looking. As you can see, it's a homemade pig made out of a plastic bleach bottle, with thread spools for legs, pink felt ears, black felt eyelashes, and a pipe cleaner for a tail. Notice this is a happy pig, for here's the great big smile, and twisted in its curly tail are some flowers.

This is a new bank I made yesterday. On the back of this pig is a coin slot. You are now going to see a first, for until now no money has been put in this piggy bank. Here goes: a quarter, a dime, a nickel, and a penny.

If I want to take the money out, I make my little pig pay through the nose. The nose is the bottle cap. Here, I'll show you. Out comes the money.

Besides buying something *we* want, there's another reason for taking the money out. To help *others*.

If we kept all our money in here, or if we took it out only for ourselves, then we could be called piggy. When I say "piggy," I don't mean to put down pigs. Having grown up on a farm, I know a lot about pigs. I raised pigs, many of them. I like pigs. There are many good things I can say about pigs, and I'm not just talking about the frying pan. But this I will say: Pigs are piggy, meaning they really care only about themselves.

We don't want to be like that. In fact, we've been taught to act differently.

Jesus said, "It is more blessed to give than to receive."

That doesn't mean we shouldn't save some of our money, but it does mean that we need to share with others. That's why we give money to the church and to other good causes.

The Bible says, "God loves a cheerful giver."

Let us pray.

Dear God: Help us learn to give in ways that would please you—by helping others. Amen.

No. 48

With Thanks

Are you hungry? Sure you are! You're like little robins, aren't you? You could eat all the time— and why not? You're growing. To grow, you need food, and when you eat you grow. So it goes—or grows.

I love to eat, and I'm already grown. Of course, if I eat too much I'll grow in the wrong places, like around the waist. But as long as I'm alive, I'll need to eat. That's the way it's supposed to be for me as well as for you.

Do you and your family sometimes go out to eat? It's fun to do that. Our family went out to eat the other evening, and I have with me the menus from the restaurant. No, I didn't steal them, I borrowed them, with the promise I'd take them back this afternoon. There are two menus in my brown bag, one for you and one for me.

As you can see, they're big and colorful. What's more—and this is what's really important—they have so many food selections. Look at how many.

From your menu—if you're choosing from the one that says "For Kids"—there's a hot dog or a hamburger with french fries. Or how about spaghetti and meatballs? Or french toast with strawberries and

116

whipped topping? Or the Big Sandwich (two pancakes, one egg, one strip of bacon, and one sausage link)? There's more, but doesn't this sound yummy?

From my menu, here's one of my favorites, an English-burger—crisp bacon strips on a slice of melted cheese over a juicy hamburger. Or I could choose a nice chef's salad, which would be ham, turkey, cheese, egg slices, and tomato wedges on crisp greens with my choice of dressing. Or there is fried chicken or steak or soup or a hearty breakfast or delicious desserts and so on.

Here are some pictures of the dishes they serve there. Makes me want to eat. How about you?

This week is Thanksgiving. On that special day, this coming Thursday, we'll eat and eat and eat. No, I won't eat at this restaurant or at any other restaurant that day, although some people will. Instead, we'll gather around a family table, where we'll eat turkey and dressing and everything that goes with it. It will be delicious.

Do you know there are people who go to bed hungry each night, even on Thanksgiving evening? And some of these aren't just hungry, they are starving. I think of this often when I go out to eat, or when the Thanksgiving meal is set and we're ready to eat. That certainly isn't a happy thought.

While we have much to eat, we also have much more for which to be thankful. I hope that this Thanksgiving Day, as we give thanks for our food, we'll also give thanks to God for the many blessings we have. But we must also ask God to help us know how best to help others who are hungry, who don't have as much to be thankful for. You can also ask your parents or your church school teacher or me—I'm always ready to talk about this with you—how you can help others this way. Here at church we often bring cans of food to share with hungry people, and at other times we share our money to help buy food for others. Would you like to do this?

Whenever you go out to eat, and when you see all that food listed in the menu, remember what we've talked about this morning. Give thanks for what we have, and offer a helping hand to those in need.

Let us pray.
Dear God: We're very thankful to you for so much, and we're very concerned for others who have so little. Amen.

No. 49

Say It with Straw

Can you keep a secret?
Good.

That's what I want you to do this week and in the coming weeks. Let me explain.

I want you to do some acts of kindness for people in your family, but I don't want them to know it was *you* who did the good deeds. That's your secret. But there's more.

In my brown bag I have something for each of you. What I have are some small plastic bags, and in each is a crib and some straw. I want you to think of this as Jesus' crib in the stable. Between now and Christmas, I want you to begin preparing the crib for Jesus by putting the straw in the crib. Sounds easy, doesn't it?

Ah, but there is only one way to do this. Listen carefully, for I want you to understand and explain it to the rest of your family. You see, they are to do this *with* you.

Take the crib and place it where it won't get knocked over. Then take the straw and put it on a plate next to the crib. Now, how does the straw get into the crib? Every time you or a member of your family does a kind deed for another family member without being caught and without telling anyone, the person who does the deed puts one straw into the crib.

What would be a kind deed? It could be making someone else's bed or putting Dad's slippers by his chair or finding something someone has misplaced and

119

returning it or getting the mail in for Mom or polishing your brother's shoes or sharpening some of your sister's pencils. The list of kindnesses is endless. Just look around for what can be done for the people in your family. And remember, don't let anyone know you're doing it.

Each week draw names, and don't let anyone know the name you draw, for that is the one for whom you'll do the good deeds all week. This way the whole family will be able both to do good deeds and receive good deeds, and they won't even know who is being so nice to them.

I want you to think of it as preparing Jesus' crib with love. That's how Jesus will know it is his crib: by the love we have put into it. The straw measures the good we've done with love.

What a way to prepare for Jesus!

I have one crib-and-straw packet for each family. So if there are two or more from the same family, let's allow the youngest to come get it. Instead of taking it to church school, leave it with your parents. OK?

Remember, do good, but keep it a secret. Let the straw speak for you, with each piece of straw being a deed of love.

When Mary and Joseph were looking for a place to stay on the night Jesus was born, the innkeeper allowed them to stay in the stable, for "there was no place for them in the inn." He could have said no. Instead he helped them. To this day, we don't know that man's name, but we do remember what he did.

No one needs to know the good deed we do for Jesus by helping others, but God will know. What a wonderful way to prepare for Jesus.

Let us pray.

Dear God: For Jesus' sake, and with love in our hearts, we'll do good deeds for others. Amen.

120

No. 50

Let Your Light Shine

Isn't the sanctuary beautiful, all decorated for Christmas!

I like the candles in the windows, the red bows, the wreaths, and the greens. It makes Christmas seem so near.

We put up our decorations at home this week. There too, Christmas is in the air.

But we had a problem. No, there's nothing wrong with our tree. It's a beauty, brought in from the forest, with full green limbs. We had no problem finding all the ornaments, for we had carefully packed them after last Christmas and stored them in the attic. We did have a problem with the lighting, though, and we didn't notice it until all the ornaments were hung and we turned on the lights and stood back to take a good look. Every light went on but one. We noticed not so much the lights that were on as the one that wasn't on. Even the ornaments appeared to fade into the tree when our attention was focused on the one bulb that didn't work.

That bulb has since been replaced.

In my brown bag I have a string of lights. I brought it to help show you what I'm talking about. Give me a few seconds to pull it out, untangle it, and plug it in.

There. Aren't the lights pretty? Wait a minute. Do you see what I see? I can tell that you are looking at the bulb that's not working—right? That's not the way it's supposed to be.

Lights on a Christmas tree mean more than decoration. They're there to tell us to let our light shine so that others can see the real meaning of Christmas.

Let's think of this unlit bulb as us when we're sad or grumpy or upset or difficult to be around or too busy to care for others. You know what I mean. We are all that way some of the time, but if that's the way we act during the Christmas season, those around us won't notice all the good things we could be saying about the true meaning of Christmas. Like you notice this bulb that's not working, they will notice the dark side of us. And that's not good.

We have so much to smile about, so much to laugh about, so much to sing about during this joyous time of the year. Sure, there are still problems in the world and in our lives. But the words from the Bible "Let your light so shine" are helpful. So let's do that— light up with the good news about God in our lives and with the good news about Jesus, whose birthday we're about to celebrate.

Let us pray.
Dear God: May our light shine and show the joyful good news of this Christmas season. Amen.

No. 51

His Star

This morning I put in my brown bag the biggest piece of yellow paper I could find.

How big is it? Oh, I'd say two feet by four feet. That ought to be big enough.

How do you like the color? No, this isn't just any pale yellow, it's bright yellow—this shouts at us. Sure gets our attention!

Now I want to show you something. Watch carefully.

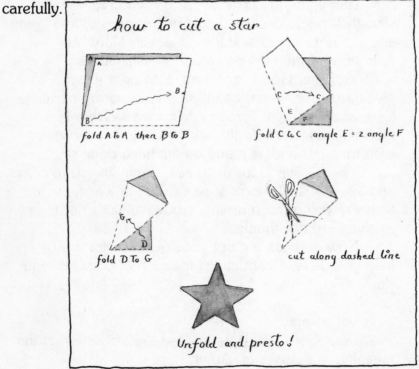

how to cut a star

fold A to A then B to B

fold C & C angle E = 2 angle F

fold D to G

cut along dashed line

Unfold and presto!

Ready? Let's see what we have here. A star.

And the wise men said, "For we have seen his star . . . , and have come to worship him." The wise men were talking about Jesus.

A star at Christmastime is expected. We see this star everywhere, and atop most Christmas trees. When we have to look up to see the star—the way the wise men saw Jesus' star—it tells us: When we come to Jesus, we need to look up and give thanks to God. After all, it was God who sent us Jesus.

In the Bible it says of Jesus' star, "And lo, the star which they had seen in the East went before them, till it came to rest over the place where the child was."

Think of this star as a way of talking about God guiding us to what is really important—Jesus. This star can remind us of him. We're wise when we come to Jesus.

And again the Bible says, "When they saw the star, they rejoiced exceedingly with great joy; and going into the house they saw the child with Mary his mother, and they fell down and worshiped him."

You see, God is directing us to do the same, to give Jesus our special attention. He is worthy of our love, and when we come to Jesus we worship him as God intends. Let's do this with great joy as those first wise men did and as many others have done since.

Yes, his star is for us to see, reminding us to come and see Jesus and to express our joy in worship—just as we're doing this morning. Above all, let's not forget to give God our thanks.

Now you can cut out your own star for Jesus. To help you, I have instructions for each of you. Make his star!

Let us pray.

Dear God: Let us never lose sight of or forget the meaning of Jesus' star. Amen.

No. 52

Do You See Jesus?

How well can you see?
     Each of you has two eyes, and as far as I know none of you has any trouble seeing. That's good. But do you see what you're looking at? Let me give you a test.

I have in my brown bag a big picture of Jesus. I'm going to put it up on this easel, and I want you to look at it and tell me if you see him. There.

Do you see Jesus? Most of you are shaking your heads sideways, and I take that to mean no. Well, let me show you where and how to look at it. Here are his eyes, here's his nose, here's his mouth, here's his forehead, here's his hair, here's . . . I know, when you first looked at this picture it looked like nothing but blotches of black and white. Now you see Jesus in the picture.

This makes me wonder if we see Jesus in life, the life that's lived around us. For example, we can see him in the help one person gives to another—say a church school teacher helping you. No, the teacher isn't Jesus, but through his or her loving actions you can see him.

Or take the person who goes out of the way to help people who are hungry, thirsty, without clothes, sick, or in prison. Jesus said, "As you did it to one of the least of these . . . , you did it to me." When one person helps another, with love, we see Jesus in that person.

We also see Jesus in the very people who need help. We see him in their eyes, saying, "Won't you help?"

We can also see Jesus in people who are trying to do what is right, what God wants—such as those who are trying to be honest, trying to be fair, trying to be caring in all they do.

Sometimes it's not easy to see Jesus in the lives of others, especially when they don't act in a loving or right way. But look again. Maybe you can see him in them too, for even through their unloving act we can see Jesus reminding us of how we could and should be more loving.

One reason we come to church is to help ourselves see Jesus better, to hear what he says to us. We see and hear him when we talk together about this. We read the Bible and talk about it. We ask for help from God in order to do this.

It's not easy, because the picture is sometimes hard to make out. But let me assure you that we can see Jesus in life. Look at the loving faces of those around you and you'll see him. Look again at the loving ways of those who have helped you and others, and you'll see Jesus. Look at your own life, when you are loving and helpful, and there too you'll see Jesus.

Yes, we see him in this picture when we learn how to look at it the right way. And we learn how to see Jesus all around us when we see people doing what Jesus taught them to do.

Now look again at this picture of Jesus. You see Jesus, don't you? Why? Because you now know how to look at it in order to see him. That's what we want to learn to do in order to see him in the lives of others. And may others see Jesus in us.

Let us pray.
Dear God: Help us to see Jesus. Amen.